THE *REALLY EASY*
STUDENT'S GUIDE

TO

MAKING MONEY

WITHOUT REALLY TRYING

BY

Sam Hall

Published by www.samhallbooks.com
December 2018

Second Edition, December 2018
Published by www.samhallbooks.com

First edition published as eBook 2018 by
Matador/Troubadour, UK and www.samhallbooks.com

To my Grandson, Peter
who introduced me to the gurus of finance and masters of
motivational oratory on YouTube when he was just 16 years
old and I? 81 years!

About Sam Hall

Sam Hall was almost 82 years old with little experience of investing when his grandson introduced him to the financial world. Inspired and intensely grateful, Hall, an author and journalist of nearly 50 years standing, decided to embark on some deep research into all aspects of saving and making money.

Realising that half the British population was in fear of never being able to escape from debt, he decided that it was time to convince young people that saving is infinitely better than spending and to show them how to create wealth. The result was *The Really Easy Student's Guide to Making Money Without Really Trying.*

As a Reuter correspondent, Hall dined with Kings and Presidents - but was subsequently forced by circumstance to live with the homeless on one of London's main railway stations. Nonetheless, his positive approach to life enabled him to extricate himself from paupery and he went on to become News Editor of Europa Magazine, Syndication Editor for Visnews and an on-screen reporter covering the top international stories of the day for ITN's prestigious flagship programme, *News at Ten.*

Travelling to more than 90 countries around the world, he has covered various wars, riots and disturbances including the Nigerian-Biafran civil war, the Turkish invasion of Cyprus and the Siege of Beirut.

A compulsive traveller, he walked as a young man from Barcelona to Copenhagen and as a middle-aged one nearly 400 miles across the French-Italian Alps in the footsteps of Hannibal, not to mention another 328 miles from his home in Surrey to Lands End – an epic journey he describes in his book *'Blisters'.*

Hall also sailed across the North Sea in an open Viking boat and travelled thousands of miles in the High Arctic. His book *'The Fourth World: The Heritage and Destruction of the Arctic'* is considered a definitive work on the Arctic for which he was likened in his writing to that of Wilfred Thessiger.

Hall is also a film-maker who, in conjunction with the Norwegian TV and film production companies, Bergefilm and Videomaker Nord, has won several international awards. Many of these films have been shown in more than 50 countries worldwide and ultimately earned him a Lifetime Achievement Award by the British company, CS Media.

Sam Hall is also an accomplished lecturer, presenter and conference host, and an acclaimed hyper-realistic artist.

-£££-

CONTENTS

INTRODUCTION

Most teenagers and student's would say they want to be rich. Right? You want a Ferrari in the garage, a house with a swimming pool, another house on a tropical island. You want to be able to fly first class, stay in top class hotels and eat in five star restaurants whenever you want.

So do I! And we can because anything - everything - is possible! If you want it enough! And you really don't have to do very much at all to achieve those goals.

Let me say straight away, this is *not* a 'Get Rick Quick Scheme'.

To make money successfully, you need patience and most importantly the discipline to ignore the latest hot tips, persuasive advertising and to avoid jumping on the emotional bandwagon of buying and selling at the wrong times.

That said, making money is actually very simple. By the time you have read the following eight points, you will know *exactly* what I have done. The rest is up to you.

You don't even have to read the rest of this book - although you will benefit enormously if you do.

Here are some suggestions as to what you might do:
1. Pay of any debts and stay out of debt for the rest of your life.
2. Save every penny, every cent, euro, krona, rupee, dollar you can.
3. When you have enough money to open an investment account, such as a Vanguard Life Strategy Fund comprised of 60% stocks and 40% bonds, add the minimum of £25 (roughly $32) or as much money as you can possibly save each month. (Incidentally, I have no connection with Vanguard or any other investment fund.

I recommend it simply because I have invested in it and like you, I want to make money, too).

4. As your money appreciates, buy more Index Funds covering stock market indexes in the UK, North America, Latin America, Europe and Asia.

5. Buy long and short term government bonds from the same geographical areas to create a balanced portfolio with a ratio of 60% stocks and 40% bonds. You can reverse the ratio later in life.

6. Ignore completely the day-to-day stock market news, economic crashes, warnings of doom and gloom in the press, and

7. Sleep well every night knowing that if you follow these suggestions, you could be earning money doing absolutely nothing else. Don't hang about. Start *now!*

That's it. Now, you know all the basic steps you should adhere to if you want to become a millionaire.

If you do, you will have a portfolio that you can leave and (apart from re-balancing, about which more later), more or less forget about for ten years or more regardless of any negative news.

Sensibly, though, you will read on and learn how to add to your portfolio, what to buy and how to allocate your purchases across different geographical areas and sectors of the business world. Now, you are on your way!

Who Is This Book Aimed At?

When I first thought of writing this book, I wanted to target it at young people between the ages of 14 and 22 years for a very simple reason: the earlier you start saving money and investing it, the more money you will make and the faster you will become wealthy.

There's a simple rule that states that unless you invest, you will never be rich (unless, of course, in the unlikely event you win the lottery or someone leaves you a million in their will!)

Putting any spare money in a savings or bank account for the long term will get you nowhere in the long term. As I said, you now know everything you *need* to know to make money, although you don't know everything you *should* know.

So stay with me and I promise I will try to turn your life around and we will all reap the benefits.

Why Believe Me?

Let's be honest, why would you or anyone else take financial advice from me?

As I write this, I am 81 years old. Until a couple of months ago, I had only very limited knowledge of the financial world.

What knowledge I did have was bad news. Like so many other people - including financial experts - I got caught up in the euphoria of a rising market, bought shares at the wrong time and then they crashed and I sold at the bottom of the market.

Later, I invested in an HSBC fund and ended up with just over £44,000, which is pretty pathetic for an 81-year-old.

Then, a year ago, I was lucky - or unlucky - enough to jump onto the Bitcoin bandwagon. At that time one Bitcoin was worth about £3,500. I decided to risk £5,000. That was in August 2017.

By December of that year, the price of one Bitcoin had shot up to £14,756 and I was sitting on £21.986 - a profit of £18,476. Talk about euphoria! I was cock-a-hoop with joy!

Timing and the Volatility of Cryptocurrencies

I should have sold out then. If I had, I'd be a lot wealthier than I am now. But cryptocurrency markets are extremely volatile - rocketing to the moon one minute and dropping like a stone the next.

It reminded my of my son, Ben, when he was about seven years old. In those days, children were allowed to visit the flight deck of an aircraft and when Ben was given the opportunity on a flight to the Greek Islands, he asked the captain what would happen 'if you run out of air'.

The captain thought for a minute and said: "I guess you become a 70-ton stone!" And that's exactly what happened with Bitcoin.

By January, 2018, the price of one Bitcoin had dropped like a Boeing-737 without air and suddenly, in just four hours overnight, the price had fallen back to just over £4,830.

Saved by the Skin of my Teeth

It was crazy. Even so, I consider myself lucky because I could have lost the lot.

So given my lack of experience in the financial world, why would I write a 'How To' book about investing and, more importantly, hope that people would believe me?

The answer lies in the Dedication to this little book.

Listen and Learn from the Masters

Peter, my grandson, is Norwegian. He lives in Sweden and is clued up about all kinds of stuff. It was he who told me about some of the amazing motivational speakers on YouTube - Les Brown, Simon Sinek, Tony

Robbins and several others. Check them out. They're inspirational!

I listened to them avidly and cannot recommend them highly enough because what they give you is self-esteem, confidence and the knowledge that *anything - everything is possible if you want it enough.*

You should repeat that every night before going to bed and every morning when you get up!

They teach you that you *will* find a way to achieve your goals and dreams; that remarkable people can do extraordinary things, whatever their age and experience.

The Wisdom of a 16-Year-Old

It was Peter, who - aged sixteen- recommended that I read a book that he had just bought called *Money: Master the Game* by Tony Robbins, one of the motivational speakers I just mentioned. .

Peter - and Tony Robbins - changed my life. I devoured this book and subsequently many other books about investing, finance and markets in general.

They all tell pretty much the same story. A story that cannot be told enough - and which mostly have not reached the attention of young people like you.

In mid-June, 2018, I made some pretty important decisions.

1.   To save every penny I could.
2.   To create an investment portfolio with Fidelity, a huge investment firm with a user-friendly website.
3.   To create standing orders from my bank directly into that portfolio - and then to forget about the investment and in ten year's time see how much profit I had made.

An Exciting Life as a Journalist and TV Reporter

Again, why listen to me? No reason really - except that during my working life I was a journalist for nearly 50 years and journalism gives you a broad outlook on life.

I worked on local newspapers, magazines and for the international news agencies, UPI, AP, AFP and Reuters, for whom I became the Chief Scandinavian correspondent based in Stockholm, Sweden.

In 1967 and 1978, I also reported from the six southern states in America and Cuba, based in Miami.

Reuters subsequently sent me to cover the Nigerian-Biafran war, flying from Lagos in Nigeria to the front line once every couple of weeks.

Later, I joined Visnews, the television arm of Reuters, covering the Northern Ireland 'troubles' in the seventies - riots, kidnapping, bombs and bullets.

In that job, I learned to write to film, which led in turn to my becoming first a scriptwriter, then a field producer and eventually an on-air reporter for 13 years with ITN's flagship news program, *News at Ten.*

From War to Adventure

During that time, I lived through some extraordinary experiences. I covered the Nigerian-Biafran civil war, the Turkish invasion of Cyprus, the Brixton riots, Paris riots and riots in Amsterdam.

During the Israeli bombing and occupation of West Beirut in 1982, I survived being bombed and shelled by land, sea and air for 17 hours a day during one nerve-racking month.

A more peaceful but equally scary story was sailing on the most authentic Viking open boat ever built across the North Sea.

Then, 90 miles off the Norwegian coast, we lost our authentic steering oar and in the middle of the night had to be rescued and towed back to Norway.

Back then, I wished fervently I could have been back home mowing the lawn!

Later, I spent three years investigating the Jeremy Thorpe affair, when the Leader of the Liberal Party was ultimately tried in the Old Bailey for conspiring to murder his alleged former homosexual lover.

Indeed, it was me that completely changed the direction of the police investigation during that case.

Finally, I worked a couple of years for TV-AM's *Good Morning Britain* programme, first as a reporter and Washington correspondent, and finally as a news presenter.

It was a thoroughly enjoyable job, not least when I was asked to cover the cricketer Ian Botham's 428 mile (713 kilometer) walk from Perpignan in France across the Alps to Turin in Italy to raise money for Leukemia.

So, all in all, you could say I've been around a bit and learnt a lot!

The Essence of Journalism - Deep Research

One thing journalism teaches you is to make incisive decisions instantly and act on them, and how to do deep research quickly.

After reading Tony Robbins' book, *Money: Master the Game,* I did just that.

I read everything I could lay my hands on about investments and the financial world, the importance of good health in the creation of wealth, how positive thinking attracts positive results and not least about student loans, buying a home and the joys of giving to others.

Most importantly, I bought a wealth calculating app

which taught me how much money it is possible to make in the long long-term whilst literally sitting back, getting on with your life and doing almost nothing

Making Decisions, Taking Action

I began to save every penny I could. I downloaded a Spending Tracker app so I could keep a record of everything I spent - and then stopped spending my money, saving it instead. You'd be amazed at how much you can save, even when you're broke!

I checked out the Morningstar website, which is loaded with tips about investing and publishes reports on markets, stocks and shares, and bonds and investment funds.

Fidelity, too, has a wealth of advice on how to generate wealth, as do many other websites. There's any amount of material out there to guide you.

The problem is that most of it is complicated - full of jargon, charts and diagrams that don't make much sense if you are a novice.

It can take years to figure out what the financial world is all about.

Worse, it is a minefield managed by a bunch of people who as often as not are more interested in making themselves wealthy with your money than making *you* rich with your own.

Even books like *Money: Master the Game* are around 650 pages long. Tony Robbins' book is full of thought-provoking facts and figures, but 650 pages is a long slog!

He also writes about the world's greatest investors and how *they* made their money and *that* is fascinating.

Many other books are frankly tedious reading. So, I've done most of the research for you and hope you will find this an easier read than other tombs on the subject.

Dean Acheson, a former American Secretary of State once described an editor as someone who sorts out the wheat from the chaff. And then publishes the chaff.

I promise not to do that. I will share with you in the simplest terms what I have learned - and especially how you can make sure that in the long term, you will never have to worry about money.

Why am Writing this Book?

When I was your age, nobody told us about money management or how to accumulate wealth and stay out of debt. There were no books to read that was aware of.

None of this was taught in schools - and still isn't, although I believe there are plans in the UK to include money management in the school curriculum at some stage in the future.

That the intricacies of finance have not been taught in schools is a scandal, because what I have learned and want to tell you is life-changing.

As I said, I am 81 and by the time this book is published I will be 82 years old. That's extremely late to start thinking about making a fortune. But I am learning, too. Every day! And I intend to share all of that with you.

As I write this, I have a portfolio with Fidelity (https://www.fidelity.co.uk/fil/home) worth £72,000. Hopefully I will live to be at least 92. I am healthy and reasonably fit and have a good chance these days of getting to 100.

By then, I would expect to have a minimum of £175,000 - and would have done very little to achieve it. I hope also that by writing this and other books, I can improve on that considerably.

Whatever the final sum is, with luck I will at least be able to leave a substantial sum to my grandson, Peter, as a 'thank you' for setting me on the right path.

So, once again, why am I writing this book?

Because I believe *passionately* that becoming wealthy is possible! And most definitely worth the effort.

You're Not the Only One Who Wants to Make Money!

I'm doing it because I, too, want to make money and invest not only in my own future - but also that of my dear wife, Susanna, and most especially in the future of my four grandchildren.

I believe that if you, as a young student, follow this guide you will become wealthy, very possibly even a millionaire. Whereas even if I live to be a hundreds years old, I will have less than 20 years in which to make money.

You, on the other hand, will have at least 50 or even more years available to you and provided you take on board some of the suggestions in this little book, that pretty much *guarantees* you millionaire status.

It's not going to happen immediately, but it *will* happen.

Slowly but surely!

All you need is a start-up amount, a lot of patience, passion and perseverance and perhaps a couple of hours of your time every six months or so to re-balance your portfolio. More on how to do that later.

You can do all this online, on your smartphone, tablet or laptop from your home.

It just couldn't be easier!

-£££-

Chapter One

THE MAGIC OF
SAVING AND COMPOUNDING

Any investor will tell you that 'compounding' is am extraordinarily powerful way of making money.

So - what is compounding? Let's say you put 25 pounds, dollars, zlotys or whatever into a bank account with no interest and therefore no compounding.

In 100 years, you would still nominally have only 25 of whichever currency is yours.

Except that you wouldn't really because during those years, if your government prints too much money as governments have done in the past, your 25 whatevers would have lost most of their value.

However, if your bank paid you just five per cent interest, in 50 years your 25 'whatevers' would be worth 287.68 'whatevers', which, as I am sure you get my drift now, I shall in future refer to as pounds sterling!

On that basis, after one year, you would have £25 plus 5% interest, one pound more. In year two, you would have £25 plus three pounds = £28.

In year three, you would have £25 plus another £4 interest to make £29. And so it goes on, year after year after year.

Again, for doing absolutely nothing. Just leaving the money in a savings bank offering a top rate of interest (the longer you leave your money alone, the higher the rate) to create more money for you. How cool is that?

```
Year  3: £25 + £   4 = £  29
Year  4: £25 + £   5 = £  30
Year  5: £25 + £   7 = £  32

          And so on, until

Year 30: £25 + £  83 = £108
Year 40: £25 + £151 = £176
Year 50: £25 + £262 = £287
Year 60: £25 + £571 = £596
```

The Magic of Compounding at 5% interest

Save as Much as You Can, as Early as You Can!

The earlier you start, the more time you have to accrue more money.

Of course, at first sight, turning £25 into £596 in 65 years doesn't seem very much. Sixty-five years into the future - as seen from the point of view of a 15 or 16 year old - is unimaginable.

Hopefully, you will just take my word for it because, actually, it's *massive!*

You Are Richer Than You Think!

These days, young people aged 11-16 years receive an *average* £12.30 a week pocket money. Some more, some less.

What's more, one in every four 14-year-olds have a part-time job - as do 34% of 14-16 year olds.

Whether you are delivering newspapers or pizzas, baby sitting, working in a shop, waiting in a restaurant or working as a stable hand, as a 16-17 year old, you would be earning approximately £3.40 an hour or, as an 18-21 year old £4.60 an hour.

Let's say that if, as a 14-16 year old, you worked three hours a day, two days a week (or vice versa). You would then be earning £32.70 a week. That's £141.70 a month or £817.50 a year.

Supposing, at that age, you saved £100 a month and left it in a bank or investment account at an interest rate of just five 5% a year.

By the time, you were 50, you would have £114,355 - and if you continued until you reached retirement age at 65, you would increase that to £264.925 - more than quarter of a million pounds.

And you would have done absolutely nothing to earn that money. That's the power of compounding.

Time is All Important

Unfortunately, all too many people know nothing about compounding.

As I said, it is not taught in schools - although it certainly should be - so many people like me only learn about it far too late in life.

Yet the difference between starting to save £100 a month at the age of 15, 21, 45 and 65 respectively is phenomenal. Let's assume that you continue to save to the age of 65, the normal retirement age:

That means the 15-year old has 50 years in which to save, At a very moderate annual interest rate of five per cent:

The 15 year old would earn £263,778 in 50 years.
The 21 year old would earn £190,440 in 44 years.
The 45 year old would earn £ 41,663 in 20 years.
The 65 year old would be too late - zilch!

But that's at only 5%. During the 10 years ending March 2018, the FTSE 100 index gave a return of 23 %.

Needless to say, as financial experts are always required to tell you, past records do not guarantee future success.

Sadly, the pundits are now forecasting a downturn to between 6%-7%. Some pessimists believe it may be as low as 4%-5% over the next ten years to 2028, but that doesn't mean there won't be another rising market later on.

There's no reason at all why previous returns of 20% or more should re-occur because the markets always follow a cyclical pattern.

Bulls and Bears

What rises to a peak (a bull market) sooner or later always falls to a trough (a bear market). It's like being at sea, riding the waves , surviving the storms and enjoying the calms. It's a cyclical process that continues indefinitely.

Most investors - including the so-called experts - let their emotions dictate when to buy and when to sell,

So they tend to buy when everybody gets excited as the prices go higher and higher, and buy near the top of the rising curve.

Then, the eternal cycle kicks in and the prices begin to drop like a 70-ton plane again.

That's when they panic and sell near the bottom of the cyclical curve. In other words, they invested to *lose* money, not gain it.

Even so, if the *average* return for the ten years to 2028 is between six and eight per cent, the 20-year-old's £100 a month compounded annually would be between £16,765 to £18,774 at the end of the ten year period.

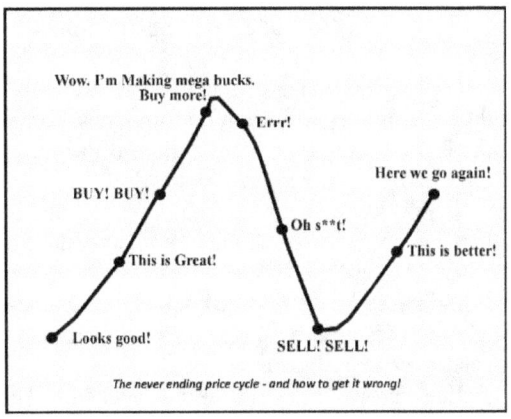

Wow. I'm Making mega bucks.
Buy more!

Errr!

BUY! BUY!

Here we go again!

This is Great!

Oh s**t!

This is better!

Looks good!

SELL! SELL!

The never ending price cycle - and how to get it wrong!

If he or she kept going until the age of 80 they would have between £678,139 (6%) and a massive £1,624,164.

No, that's not a mistake. It's a *ginormous* return that makes our 20-year-old a millionaire. For doing almost nothing! And that is just on the £100 going in every month, month after month, a sum that over the coming years, you could increase dramatically.

How? Well, obviously, as 15-year-olds reach their 20s, 30s, 40s and 50s, they are going to be earning much more and would therefore be able to hive off a great deal more than £100 from their monthly salary.

In fact, if they increased their £100 by even £25 a month every time they were given a raise in salary, they'd make their million much, much earlier. And think how quickly you would reach millionaire status if the average interest rate returned to 20%.

So, now you can see why starting to save as early as possible is really important.

The Cost of Spend, Spend, Spend!

If only more young people knew about all this, life would be completely different for thousands, perhaps hundreds of thousands or even millions of people.

Instead, they *spend* their money.

There is a school a mile from my home and between 3.30pm and 4pm, school children of all ages pour out from their classes.

And guess what? A large number of them head straight for Tesco Express, which has shelves laden with chocolates, candies and crisps.

Others crowd into KFC to buy chicken and chips or into the local chippie. All *spending* money.

Until very recently, I was the same. If it is not raining, snowing or I am abroad or ill, I routinely walk five miles a day to stay healthy.

Not infrequently, I would stop at a coffee shop called Fothergills, where you can sit in comfortable armchairs and sofas and read the day's newspapers at no cost.

Drinking Money Cost Me £452 a Year!

It was a great way to break my walk and what's more, the women serving in this little shop made a fantastic Mocha - a mixture of coffee and chocolate which gives you a double-whammy kick. It was brilliant!

Then, after my grandson, Peter, told me about the book by Tony Robbins, I realized that I was paying £2.90 for my Mochas - three times a week.

So I did some sums. I was spending £8.70 a week - or more scary still, £452 a year! And if, even at the age of 81, I invested that at 8% for ten years, I would get £7,071.

That would pretty much pay for my own funeral. Instead, I would have drunk more than seven grand's worth of money!

Five Terrible CCCCCs:
Crisps, Chocolate, Coffee, Chicken and Chips

If you are over 18 and have a regular job, the likelihood is that you will spend at least part of your salary on sandwiches at lunchtime or a coffee in your local Costa or Starbucks.

It is the beginning of a life cycle and it reminds me of a story I used to tell my granddaughter, Coco:

"On a dark and stormy night there were three pirates sitting in a cave and one said: 'Jim, tell us a story'. And Jim said: 'On a dark and stormy night, there were three pirates sitting in a cave...'" and so on and on and on.

It's the same in life. You go to the office, shop or factory or clean windows or do gardening, and you work day in, day out. You pay your monthly household bills and you spend your money. Indeed, you *have* to go to work in order to pay your bills and spend your money, and ... It's that never-ending cycle again.

The problem is that we are besieged by advertising. Wherever we go, companies are trying to sell you their product.

Buy two, get one free. There are all kinds of enticements. They pop up on your smartphone, on your laptop or tablet and on television.

Did you know that for the most part, half-hour programmes on television in the UK are only 21 minutes long and one-hour programmes just 43 minutes long?

In other words, there are nine minutes of advertising in every half-hour programme and 21 minutes in an hour's programme.

In the U.S., there's so much advertising that by the time they've finished you've forgotten what you were watching.

There's no escape. You can't go anywhere these days except possibly into the depths of the countryside or the middle of a swamp without seeing advertisements.

Retailers tell you that you *need* these products to improve your health or your looks. Or to satisfy your desires for fashionable clothes, fast cars, food, fizzy drinks, sweets, clean wash basins, laundry and other luxuries.

This incessant bombardment is hard to resist.

You Do *Not Need* These Luxuries! Remember - It is the Companies That Make the Money - Not You!

Everyone, it seems, wants your money. And the fact is, the more you earn, the more you are likely to spend - a snazzy car to boost your ego, a pair of Jimmy Choo shoes, a new top, signature shirts costing £160 a time, an Armani suit, meals out, theatres, golf clubs - the list is endless.

Even a pint at the pub is an average £6 now and some people down half a dozen pints - £36. Guess what? If you do that once a week for 50 years, you would have boozed away £1,070,792 (at 8% annual interest). More than a million pounds! Even if you only had three pints a week, you would have drunk well over half a million pounds.

That's all fine *after* you've made your fortune and can afford it. But ultimately, a lifetime of spending leads to an endless, lifetime struggle to make ends meet.

For example, most school children and students wouldn't bother to buy sunglasses. They can't afford it.

A young person earning, let's say, £10,000 a year, might splurge on a basic pair of sunglasses costing £25-£40 at SpecSavers or Boots .

The 30-35 year old manager of a company, however, might well be happy to spend £125 on a pair of designer glasses.

Creaming off the Top

So its time to decide whether you want to save and invest or be a spender. The fact that you are reading this book suggests the former. So how best to go about it?

When I was a boy, I used to help the milk girl deliver milk on her daily rounds. In those days, we bough milk in one pint glass bottles.

There were several different kinds of milk but the top 20% of the bottles I remember comprised a wonderfully rich, yellow cream. They were known as 'Gold Top' bottles.

As a teenager, the moment you get a job, whether it is just part-time or full time, you should cream off a certain amount of money *before* you pay any bills to anyone else.

The same applies to everyone, no matter how old they are.

It is something you should do throughout your life. The trick is not to take too much - or too little.

How much is that? That's a question I can't answer. You could start with not less than 10%. In the long run, the best amount would probably be 15%.

That money goes, with every pay cheque, every month, without fail into your savings or investment account - and we will discuss which is the better later on.

Three Simple Tasks to Set Yourself Up

If you haven't done so already, your first task is to set up a current account and a savings account at your local bank.

Make sure you pay your cheque or pocket money (depending on whether you are working or not) into your current account and use that account to bank your personal 15% (or whichever amount you choose). Then transfer it directly via a standing order into your savings or investment account, and only then use the remaining balance to pay your bills.

That way you will learn to budget with what you have left.

Secondly, as I mentioned at the outset, as soon as you have enough money in the bank - probably in the region of £1000 - open an investment ISA account with an investment company.

There are dozens of such companies - Hargreaves Lansdown, Franklin Templeton, Vanguard, Fidelity, Schroder, Schwab and so on.

Personally, I use Fidelity (*fidelity.co.uk*) because they have a really user friendly website. Not that I am rewarded in any sense by being a flag flyer for them.

We will discuss ISA's later on. Suffice to say for the moment that you will not be taxed on the annual maximum annual allowable £20,000 or on the profits that you make in your ISA account -- and taxes are a very important aspect of your journey to lifelong wealth. We'll discuss that later on, too.

Thirdly, once you have set up an investment account, establish a Direct Debit for £25 (or more if you can afford it) to be drawn from your savings account each month. You can do this very easily from the *fidelity.co.uk* website.

Standing Orders and Direct Debits

The beauty of Standing Orders and Direct Debits is that the money is drawn from your account automatically on the same date each month. If you need to change the amount or the date, you can do that later.

Incidentally, a standing order is a regular payment that you can set up to pay other people, organisations or transfer to other bank accounts. You can amend or cancel the standing order and when you like.

A Direct Debit can only be set up by the organisation to which you're making the payment. This is obviously the better option because it takes away the temptation of changing a standing order to suit your immediate needs.

They both mean that you never see the money. After a couple of months, you will forget that you ever had it. But it will be there, slowly earning money for you in the background. Now you really are making money while doing nothing. You could, of course, lose money, but I'll show you later how to hedge against that.

It's *vital* that you do make your payments automatic and *never* miss a month. If you do, you will ultimately forfeit big money because the missed month will have a negative effect your compounding.

Can't save? Won't Save?

At this stage, most people would argue that they really can't afford to set aside 15% of their salary before paying their bills. They are up to their eyeballs already - maybe even in debt.

The answer is that actually, they *can* afford it. It's just that they don't realise that they can. If that is your argument, you need to ask yourself some serious questions.

For instance, do you smoke because others of your friends smoke? Because it looks and feels cool? Answer: Quit.

A packet of cigarettes in Britain now costs £8.26, of which nearly 80% is tax.

So apart from the fact that you are giving £6.61 to the government every time you buy a pack of fags, cigarettes are addictive, so in a couple of years you would almost certainly be smoking a pack a day.

That's £57.82 a week, or £3,006.64 a year, of which you are just handing £2,405.31 to the taxman.

How dumb is that? And given that cigarettes are proven to give you cancer, chances are you won't have time to make a fortune, anyway!

Maybe you'll say: "I can't quit". Or more likely: "I don't want to quit, I like smoking."

Okay, that's fine by me. You are the loser - but, come on, who wants to be a loser?

Never Give Up Smoking. Just Don't Smoke!

Years ago, when I was in my 30s and 40s, I smoked 25-30 cigarettes a day.

If the telephone rang, my hand would reach out to pick up the receiver (this was before the days of mobile phones), then as an afterthought I would withdraw it, quickly reach for my packet of fags, light up and only *then* pick up the phone.

It became a habit, just as smoking itself had become a habit.

One day, I was coming out of Oxford Street tube station in London and suddenly began coughing. Being a well brought up kind of guy, I put my hand to my mouth.

Then I saw that it was covered in blood!

That scared the life out of me.

However, by pure chance, that morning, there was a short article on the front page of the *Daily Mail,* about a new clinic that had opened up to teach people how to stop smoking.

Even better, it was only a few hundred meters away from the ITN headquarters where I worked.

So, during the lunch break I went there. There were two retired doctors. One said: "Do you have a lighter?"

"Sure," I said. "A gold Ronson!"

He said: "Let me have it. I'll keep it for you for six

months. Then you can have it back - although you won't need it then."

I wasn't exactly happy about that. It was a very expensive lighter. But eventually I handed it over.

The doctor then said: "Only you can stop smoking. I can't really help you…"

I thought: "Well, what the heck am I doing here then? And then he said: "All I can tell you is this: *Never, ever* say that you have 'given up' smoking. If you do, you will start again.

"Say instead: 'I don't smoke!' - then you will never smoke again. That's the psychological difference between the two."

The doctors wished me good luck - and reminded me. "You don't smoke! It's that simple."

After that, I would deliberately sit in the smoking carriage of the train going home, just to get used to not smoking in a smokers' environment.

I put on weight - a lot of weight - and, according to my wife, Sue, I was pretty grumpy for a year. But I never smoked again. I gradually lost the weight and hopefully I stopped being grumpy.

The lesson here is that if you say to yourself and others: "I don't smoke", you won't smoke.

It's the same if you say, every morning, "I'm going to be much, much richer than I am today" - then you will be wealthy. You simply have to convince your own mind. Then you can do *anything* - . And remember: *anything - everything* - is possible.

Eating Out, Eating Money

Maybe you are one of those people who head straight for KFC or MacDonald's for a quick 'snack' or cheap meal.

I did a little quick research into KFC. Some of their

family meals now cost £10.99 and even £12.99 depending on how many pieces of chicken you have.

A KFC mini breast fillet snack - a favourite among the school kids - will cost you £2.99 or if you have a carbonated drink with it, £3.99. Call it four pounds.

Eat a meal deal like that five times a week and two things are guaranteed. You will put on weight and you will have eaten £20 a week or £1,040 a year. Need I say more?

It doesn't matter who you are. The same applies whether you are in your 20s and 30s, or maybe married, perhaps with a couple of children.

Imagine how much you could save if you ate out once every couple of weeks rather than twice a week, at a cheap and cheerful restaurant, the local Indian, maybe, instead of a 'posh' restaurant with an expensive menu.

Saving Does Not Mean Total Denial

You say you can't save money? Sure you can. You'd soon get used to eating out less often because, like not smoking, it would become a habit.

Let's not forget that if you set aside 15% off your salary *before* you pay your bills, you still have 85% of your salary which you can spend on essentials and save some money.

All this may sound as if I am a killjoy - someone who says you have to deny yourself the little luxuries of life.

That's not true.

If you manage your money properly, set yourself a budget and live within it, you can still save enough from that 85% to pay your bills *and* enjoy the odd treat.

The difference is that if you make those small sacrifices now, you will have more than enough money to do what you want, when you want, and as often as you want later on because you will be wealthy, instead of constantly penny pinching because you are poor.

One of the best ways of keeping a check on what you spend is to download a free Spending Tracker app.

You simply enter in the amount of money you have available for the month, then add in every single item you buy.

The app does the rest.

It keeps a running total of what you have spent and what you have spent it on -- eating out, entertainment, fuel, gifts, holidays, groceries, travel etc. So, it is easy to see how much you have left and where you may need to cut down your expenditure.

So Let's Get Going. Start Investing *Now!*

In Britain, you need to be 18 years old to be able to open a normal bank account. It's the same in other countries, for example the United States, where you would need to open a 'custodial account' with an adult - usually a parent - if you are under 18.

However, there are several banks in the UK that offer accounts specifically for 11 to 18 year olds.

These include:

The Santander 123 Mini Current Account (up to 18 years)
The Bank of Scotland Under 19s Account
Lloyds Under 19s Account
Natwest Adapt Account (11-18 years)
TSB Under 19s Account
Ulster Bank Adapt Account (11-18 years)
Danske Bank Discovery (11-17 years)
HSBC MyAccount (11-17 years)
Nationwide FlexOne Account (11-17 years)
Barclays BarclayPlus (11-15 years)

These banks mostly pay interest - but not much! At the time of writing, the majority pay between 1% and 1.5%. The TSB Under 19s Account pays 2.5% AER on sums up to £2,000.

Some pay no interest at all - so make sure you check.

At the moment, Santander pay the best rate - 3% AER on up to £2000.

AER? What's That?

AER (short for Annual Equivalent Rate. It assumes that you keep your money in a particular savings account for at least one year.

The AER rate is superior to the *gross rate*, which doesn't take into account the all important *compound interest*.

In any event, once you have an account to suit your age, you are then in a position to create Direct Debits.

You can then invest in an Index Fund (more on those later on) with an Investment Company like Vanguard, Fidelity, Hargreaves and Lansdown etc. as quickly as you can.

Why? Because these have the potential to earn you much more money than the average miserable interest paid by the banks.

Stocks, Shares, Bonds, Index Funds?
They're Simpler Than You think!

To begin with, you might find an Equity Index Fund a safe haven for your money.

As a purely personal preference, I invested in a Vanguard 60% Equity Index Fund, which means the fund consists of 60% shares in companies and 40% in bonds.

Shares in companies - whether in the UK, America, Europe or Asia tend to be unpredictable, rising and falling quickly. It's known as 'volatility'.

Bonds are essentially a promise made by governments and other institutions to pay you a fixed rate of interest over a specific length of time.

These are mostly very stable and tend to counter-balance the volatility of stocks and shares.

Thus, a mix of stocks and bonds in an index fund is good protection.

When you are young, you would probably opt for a 60%-40% fund as stocks (shares) are more 'aggressive' in the quest to earn more money.

When you are older, you might prefer the 40% - 60% option, bonds offering a steadier, less aggressive growth rate and thus a better protective 'hedge' against the markets falling. Remember - markets always do and always will because, as we have seen, they constantly follow a cyclical pattern.

Accumulation of Income Funds?

Index Funds, which we will study in more depth later on, are in my view infinitely better than stocks because instead of just owning a small handful of shares (in different companies), an investor actually owns a small part of *every* company in the index.

Investing in an Index fund that tracks the main financial indicators, such as the FTSE 100, means that you have a small share of as many as 500 different companies at the same time. And the good news is that these days, many funds only require an initial investment of as little as £25.

Incidentally, when you do buy into an Index Fund, make sure it is an 'accumulation' rather than an 'income' fund.

Accumulation means that the dividends paid by companies in the fund are re-invested automatically, thus regularly boosting your compounding capital.

With an Income Fund, you receive a cash dividend to supplement your income. That's something you would think about much later on in life.

For the time being - reinvest your money in an accumulation fund. It's a neat way of saving and you will reap the benefits later.

Certainly, Sir. We'd be delighted to give you a Debit Card

The bad news is that all the banks will give you a Debit Card - and probably a credit card, as well. 'Free' of charge, of course. They do this because Debit cards and credit cards especially mean that the bank earns more than you do!

So be very, very careful because this is temptation wrapped up as a free gift called 'convenience'.

It means that all you have to do is walk into a shop, buy something you fancy and just 'show' your card to the shop's card machine. The amount is then *automatically* deducted from your account. *Danger! Danger! Danger!*

Always Pay Off Credit Cards Monthly

At this stage of your life, my advice would be to cut any kind of credit card up and throw it away.

If you *do* decide to use it, make <u>*absolutely sure*</u> that you pay off your debts at the end of the month.

With *no* exceptions! Always. For the rest of your life.

Because as you will see in the next chapter, debt is

the one thing you need in your life like a knife in your gut.

In the meantime, you might like to download an app called 'Wealth Calculator'.

Simply enter in the initial investment you made into it, then how much you plan to invest monthly.

The app will then calculate exactly how much you will be worth in x number of years and at the rates of interest you choose. A sensible rate would be 6%-7%. A cautious rate would be 4%-5%.

The app will then show you not only how much money you will make, but also how your much your investments will grow year on year.

You will also be able to see how, with time, the interest you earn outstrips your original and ongoing investments.

You will be amazed, thrilled and determined to follow this path to lifelong riches.

So, what have you learnt so far?

When we set out on this journey, I asked you to take a leap of faith and believe me. If you stayed with me, this is what you have learnt:

1.   How compounding makes money while you do nothing.

2.   That the earlier you start saving, the more money you make. That when you add up your pocket money and earnings from a part-time job, you are richer than you thought.

3.   That when you invest, don't let your emotions interfere - be patient and buy when prices are low.

4.   The real cost of spending. How compounding can work for you - or against you.

5.   The importance of avoiding the five CCCCCs.

6.   That advertising makes money for the

companies placing the ads - not for you.

7.   To cream 10-15% of your income off the top and pay it into your savings or investment accounts before paying any bills - then make extra savings to keep up with the bills.

8.   Why direct debits take the pain out of savings - because you don't miss the money.

9.   That you 'don't smoke' just because your mates smoke. They may laugh at you but they are the losers.

10. That saving money does _not_ mean denying yourself of the good things in life completely.

11. That by saving just £100 a month now, you could have quarter of a million pounds by the time you are 65 - all for doing nothing!

12. To download the spending tracker app -- and start saving in a current account at your bank right now.

13. When you have enough money to open an investment account, transfer at least £25 a month by Direct Debit to an Investment ISA account (a Roth IRA in the United States) at an investment company of your choice as soon as possible.

You can do all these things because anything - everything is possible!

-£££-

Chapter Two

THE DANGERS OF DEBT

If you want to be wealthy, there are two golden rules:

Never get into debt
If you *do* get in debt, *GET OUT FAST*.

There are two kinds of debt. Good debt and bad debt.

If you take a loan at, say, 4% interest and then re-invest it at 8%, that's good debt because you are using the bank or lender's money to finance your own investments.

It's called leveraging and in the right circumstances it can be a very useful way of boosting your portfolio and therefore your income or capital growth.

Of course, that kind of deal isn't easy to come by.

What is easy to come by is bad debt. The kind of debt you incur when you borrow money to buy consumer goods with your credit card.

Back in the dark ages, it used to be called 'Hire Purchase'. It was the reason why my Father refused absolutely to have a television set or a washing machine in the house.

If you were on a salary of less than £1000, as he was in those days, you could only buy a television, washing machine or a refrigerator on what we called the 'Never, Never'.

In other words, you never, never paid. Or that's the way it seemed. In fact, it was a fool's paradise and happily my father was smart.

He knew that the result could be untold stress and

distress.

Compounding Can Work Against You, Too

We've seen how the miracle of compounding can work for you, but the reality of life is that while compounded *savings* can ensure wealth for your lifetime, compounded *debt* can similarly ensure a lifetime of misery trying to pay it off .

Most credit card companies charge interest on loans at an outrageous 18.9% to 20.9% APR (Annual Percentage Rate). Some charge even more.

The APR is the rate of interest you have to pay to get the loan, including any other charges that the credit card company chooses to apply.

In other words, if you bought a laptop for £1000 and paid for it with a credit card. At 18.9%, you would have to pay a whopping £189.00 interest if you kept the loan and paid it off in full at the end of a year.

However, if you only paid off the minimum amount each month you would be debited with £25.75 each month.

According to the Debt Advisory Centre, it would take *five years and one month* to pay off this amount -- and you would end up paying more than half the original amount - £509 - in interest.

That's why it is so easy to get into debt. Just one day's shopping could result in years of being 'in the red'.

Clearly, the more you pay each month, the less you pay in interest.

For example, if you paid £30 a month, it would take two years and 10 months and the interest would be £217. That is significantly less! If you paid £45 a month, you would be back 'in the black' within two years.

So, the lesson is that if you buy a laptop, an Apple or Samsung smartphone, a bike or an X-box on a credit card, you are diving headlong into a quicksand of debt.

And if your parents buy you these things with a loan or a credit card, so are they!

Of course, if you pay off the full amount in the first month, you will pay no interest at all.

Sadly, too few people do that. So, get smart. Ask yourself if you really *need* these things - and if you do, be patient.

If you are saving and get even a 2% return on your money, why would you opt to pay 18.9% interest on a credit card loan?

Far better to wait until you have saved enough money to buy your laptop or smartphone in one go. You'd get much more satisfaction from it, too!

So, if you *do* buy with a credit card, pay off the debt at the end of the month. If you are in debt, pay off the credit card first. If you have debt on several credit cards, pay off the biggest debt first.

You might not have any money left to invest - but at least you would not have *lost* any money.

Pretending To Be Rich

So far, we have seen how saving regularly and investing wisely for the rest of your life *will* make you a fortune.

Unfortunately there are three elements that can destroy that reality.

The first is debt. The second is taxation. The third is a mix of temptation and emotion.

There are towns like Puerto Banus in southern Spain where you can see sunburned guys driving Ferraris and Porches, wearing open necked silk shirts and the latest fashion in sunglasses costing £150-£200 a time, not to mention gold bracelets and Rolex watches.

These creepy characters drive up and down the marina waterfront, showing off in front of likeminded sunburned women wearing the same fashionable sunglasses, Jimmy Choo shoes and handbags that cost anywhere up to £1000.

That's fine if you have already made your fortune and can afford to spend that kind of money without noticing it.

But all too often, these people are just pretending to be rich. And that's really not a smart thing to do if you paid for your watch, shoes, shirt, handbag and sunglasses on a credit card and your flashy car with a loan from the bank.

That's the road to financial disaster - even bankruptcy.

The Poison of Minimum Payments

I can't stress enough that over-using a debit or credit card or allowing your bank account to be overdrawn is the dumbest thing you can do because banks and credit institutions really punish people that get into debt. So, I can't repeat enough:

Always make sure that you pay the total amount off at the end of the month.

Never just pay off the minimum amount allowed.

Remember credit card companies *want* you to be in debt. Because your debt is their profit.

Half the Population Risk Being In Debt for the Rest of their Lives

One survey of 2000 British adults found that some 200 of them had spent the full amount of the available credit on their credit cards. As many again had overdrawn their bank accounts in the previous year.

Even worse, 33% of the interviewees said they were planning to take on *additional* debt on their credit cards, loans on their cars and on their mortgages.

Sometimes, they use one credit card to pay off the debt on other cards.

A similar study by the Financial Conduct Authority (FCA) showed that more than four million people in Britain are already in serious financial difficulty.

Hardly surprising then that more than *six million* Britons believe they will *never* be able to get out of debt and that fully *half* the population are *at risk* of being in debt *for the rest of their lives.*

And those in the greatest danger are 25-34 year olds!

It's the penalty people pay for spending more than they can afford. And all because at an earlier stage of their lives they spent money as if there was no tomorrow, rather than saving it for the future.

Unfortunately for them, there *is* a tomorrow and eventually it comes round today!

The Never-Ending Misery of Debt

Think what this does to people. Their lives become a constant worry.

They are harassed by debt collectors.

They receive threatening, phone calls from creditors.

They are embarrassed by having their credit cards declined when they try to pay at the supermarket check-out desk.

They have to pay hefty charges for being overdrawn at the bank.

In desperation, they borrow from friends and family - and then can't pay them back.

They spend their lives dreading bills they know they can't pay.

Spend, Spend, Spend and Keep Everyone Happy Except Yourself

Advertising combined with temptation is an invitation to dive headlong into the depths of despair.

Every company, every bank, every credit institution, every retail outlet, fast food shop, restaurant and sales person on the planet wants you to buy, buy, buy, spend, spend, spend.

It's what keeps them going. It's also what keeps the national economy going.

Consider this: The average person in Britain is now a humungous £8,000 in debt - not including mortgages. In the United States, the figure is $8,400.

To pay off £8,000 at the monthly minimum of £5 or 1% of the balance plus interest whichever is greater, would take you 35 years and cost you £11,435 in interest.

Yes, that's right. *Thirty-five* years!

That's assuming you add no further debt to the card, that the interest rate stays the same and excludes any default charges or annual card fees.

Makes you think, doesn't it? But now you can see why getting into credit card debt is a big No-No - and paying off at the minimum rate is a sure fire guarantee to a lifetime of poverty.

No wonder half the British population believe they will never get out of debt in their lifetimes!

Buy One, Get One Free. Free? Really?

Whenever you see a 'Buy one Get One free' offer, ask yourself *why* the supermarket or shop is making that offer.

Answer: They face massive competition so they need to persuade and tempt you to buy *their* product, whether you want or need it or not.

That 'free' one, of course, isn't free at all.

The supermarket or shop manager may not make a profit on the 'free' one, but at least he or she has covered the basic cost -- and thanks to the 'special' offer, you are buying from the manager's outlet rather than someone else's. And in all probability, once you are that shop you will spend money on other items.

The problem is, it is just so easy to get tempted - and not all 'free' offers are what they seem.

For example, if a sales person suggests you could save 10% on a purchase of say £75 if you sign up to their store charge card, you would almost certainly say to yourself: "Wow, why not? That's £7.50 just for signing!

Then, a little later, you go to the same store and buy goods for £100. What you wouldn't necessarily realise - until you get the bill - is that the store card is pretty much the same as a credit card.

The interest rate will be around 18%, a shade less than a credit card perhaps. Even so, if you opted to pay only the minimum, once again it would take you years to pay it off.

In other words, you took a £7.50 'gift' so that you could spend years in debt to the store.

'Fat Cats' Live off Your Money

Never forget, too, that your 'friendly' bank is a commercial, even mercenary, enterprise. They need to make money to pay their employees - and they need to make a lot of money to pay their senior managers.

The top men in the banks and in the bank's departments earn huge salaries - in some cases millions of pounds a year.

It is the same with major companies. In the year 2017-2018, the salaries of Britain's chief executives soared by 11 per cent with the average salary for these fat cats just a little less than £4 million a year.

That compares with a 2% increase for full time workers.

In 2018, at Persimmon, one of the largest house builders in the UK, the boss Jeff Fairburn received *$47.1 million* - more than 20 times his pay in 2016. Nothing fair about that. The employees got burned, though.

Fairburn gets 3,195 times as much pay as the workers. The company employs. And it was precisely those people who helped the company generate a 5% rise in its revenues during the first half of 2018. How Fairburn lives with himself is anybody's guess.

Simon Peckham of Melrose Industries received £42.8 million. That was 43 times his previous year's salary of less than a million. *Forty-three times!*

That is 1,475 times as much as a worker earning the 2018 average wage of £29,000 a year.

What did this individual actually *do* in that one year to earn that kind of obscene money

No wonder 'ordinary' people and the press call these executives 'fat cats'.

Bank managers want you to have your money in their bank so that they can charge and even penalize you for using their services. Sometimes, they 'own' your money for longer than you do - and thus get more interest on it than you do.

Ask yourself why, when you want to move money from one bank to another, it takes *five days* to make the transfer.

Five days! When we are living in a digital age and payment on a credit card transfer can be made instantly - simply by flashing your card in front of the card machine or paying online.

Answer: Because the banks can take profits on your money during that time by playing the currency markets.

Governments - and the taxman particularly - don't

like you to have cash because it means they lose control over your money.

That's because in a cash economy, you can pay your window cleaner, builder, gardener or house cleaner in cash - with the result that the tax man misses out on the taxes that otherwise would be due.

These are taxes the government and local councils need to pay for roads, railways, street lighting, garbage collection, police and fire services, and so on.

Banks don't like you to have cash, either. They don't make any money from cash - unless it is in their bank!

Closing the ATMs

And where do we mostly get cash from? ATMs - Automatic Teller Machines. Banks in the UK are currently closing ATMs at a rate of 500 a month and, according to newspaper reports, at least 10,000 ATMs are now at risk of closure in the UK.

Most of these are run by independent machine operators. Banks don't like having to pay them what are known as 'interchange' fees, but if these fees are reduced, the independent operators say they will have to close down yet more and more ATMs.

This could have a devastating effect, especially in rural areas, not least because according to the Bank of England, some 45 per cent of all transactions in the UK are in cash - and the value of cash in circulation in the UK is currently higher than ever.

What About My Pocket Money?

Of course, there are always two sides to a coin. The taxman may not want you to pay your window cleaner and gardener in cash, but if people can't get hold of cash, how will they give their kids pocket money?

Or put a pound coin in a charity collectors tin box on the High Street?

Despite these closures, the Bank of England insists that there are some 5,000 more cash machines in Britain now than three years ago - about 70,000 altogether.

Even so, there are signs that the age of cash is drawing to a close and that in future we will be reliant entirely on cash cards.

Are We Gradually Becoming A Cashless Society?

Payment with credit and debit cards is becoming ever more prevalent.

Wherever you go these days, you can pay up to £30 just by 'showing' your card to a shop's card reader.

Almost all charities now have websites on which you can make contributions by Direct Debit.

Even churches are beginning to accept contributions by credit or debit card.

Pretty much all taxis now take card payments.

Schools are increasingly going cashless, forcing parents to top up their children's cards.

Of course, gardeners, cleaners and window cleaners don't have card machines. They don't want them, either. They want payment in cash so they don't have to pay taxes.

Nor do they like being paid by cheque because cheques (checks, if you are an American) can be traced!

This is not just a trend. Britons are now spending more than four and a half *billion* pounds a month simply by flashing their cards across card machines.

And they do it more than 450 million times a month.

"We Don't Accept Cash"

Many years ago, I lived in Coconut Grove on the outskirts of Miami, Florida. When I first arrived there, I didn't have an American bank account or a credit card, so when I tried to pay cash in a local store, I was treated like a criminal.

Store owners wanted to know why I didn't have a card. They were incredulous. How could anybody *not* have one?

Time after time, I had to explain that I had only just arrived in the country - an explanation that made them even more suspicious.

Of course, even as a foreign resident, I had no problem getting a credit card once I had set up a bank account.

It is now the same in Sweden. As my grandson, Peter, who lives there will tell you, it is rapidly becoming almost impossible to spend cash in Sweden now.

One of the most common sights in Stockholm and other towns, is the shop sign reading: "We don't accept cash".

What? No More Notes and Coins?

In fact, Sweden is the most cashless society in the world. Ninety-nine per cent of all transactions are now made with plastic. Even for the tiniest amounts.

Even the High Street banks in Sweden refuse to touch cash any more. The very idea of paying cash into the bank or withdrawing it is now out of the question.

They don't accept cheques, either - and, needless to say, they have increased the fees if you want to transfer money from one account to another, or from one bank to another.

After all, that's why they want a cashless society. So they have complete control over your money and how you spend it.

When they have all that information, they make even more money by selling it on to commercial companies, who can then target you with persuasive advertising to get you to spend more of your money - for their benefit.

What this means, though, is that bus companies, for example, have increasingly banned the use of coins on their buses - ostensibly because of 'the risk to drivers'. 'Elf 'n' Safety' strike again? It makes you wonder!

Museums like the Abba Museum in Stockholm won't take cash, either, which causes a problem for many tourists.

You even have to use a card to enter public toilets, which can be embarrassing if you are on a cruise, in the country for only a day and have left your credit card on the ship.

Shop owners like the idea, though, because it lessens the risk of robberies - and it is also much faster. When you pay with a card, they don't have to fiddle about giving change with notes and coins, any more.

The Problems and Challenges of Online Payments

These advances in the way we pay for things isn't always popular.

When you can only pay for a cup of coffee with a card or a smartphone, it's a problem if you are elderly and don't have a smartphone or know how the internet works.

Approximately 85% of 16-74 year-olds in Sweden bank online or, to put it another way, 15% of elderly people do not, or don't know how to do so.

There is one overall worrying problem, though. Card machine and online payments are only possible thanks to the Internet.

And there is more fraud online now than ever.

Hackers can break into the supposedly secure internet accounts of banks and commercial companies - and steal not only masses of personal information but also vast amounts of money.

Hackers recently broke into the British Airways computer systems and stole the credit card details of thousands of people who had booked flights and paid for them with a card online. They even managed to get the expiry dates and the three-digit security number on the back.

That meant the hackers could buy whatever they wished and set up false direct debits to people's bank accounts, thus potentially stealing millions of pounds.

Bitcoin and other cryptocurrencies are another classic example. Crypto exchanges are frequently hacked and billions of Bitcoin have been stolen - some believe by North Koreans.

What all this means is that with card payments becoming almost inevitable, you have to be *even more* careful.

That's why you should always pay off your monthly debt immediately and use a spending app to keep a check on how much you are spending. If you want to be wealthy, don't ever let your spending overtake your income. And never forget the two Golden Rules.

Never get into debt
If you do get in debt, GET OUT FAST.

But What About Student Loans?

Both parents and students alike are often terrified at the mere mention of a student loan. The very words conjure up an image of tens of thousands of pounds debt which cannot be paid off for 15, 20 even 30 years.

In fact, there is absolutely no need to worry. Student

loans are okay and you certainly should not be *frightened* off going to University because you felt you would need a student 'loan' to do so.

Of course, you may feel that you don't *need* to go to university and that instead of taking on a student loan, you could actually save money from your wages and invest it.

That said, a student 'loan' - and note the inverted commas' - is very different from getting into debt with credit cards, bank or other loans.

In fact, in some respects a student 'loan' isn't really a loan at all. It's more like a donation towards your education because in the UK, you only repay it after you've graduated - and you pay nothing if you earn less than £25,000 a year.

Moreover, the repayments don't increase if you borrow a larger sum and no matter how much you earn, the 'debt' is wiped clean after 30 years.

So if it isn't a debt, what is it?

In some respects, a student 'loan' is a kind of tax. What you receive is 'tax paid' - deducted at source in exactly the same way as all income tax.

Nor do student 'loans' affect your credit rating, so you certainly won't be harassed by debt collectors.

More importantly, with student 'loans', there is no downward spiral into deeper and deeper debt such as that caused by the shamefully high interest rates charged by credit card companies.

In fact, when it comes to borrowing money a student 'loan' is probably the best deal you will ever get.

In that case, how much can I borrow - and how much do I have to repay?

Universities can charge a maximum of £9,250 for full-time students and £6,935 for part-time students.

That said, most universities charge a flat £9,000. However, those figures may well increase with inflation in the future.

The amount you can borrow depends on several factors.

These include the type of course you are studying, where you live, where you plan to study and your 'household income'.

That's the combined income of *everyone* sharing a particular place of residence.

It includes every form of: salaries and wages, retirement, profits on investments - the lot!.

According to the UK government website and MoneySavingExpert.com, you would be eligible for the maximum amount only if your household income is less than £25,000 a year, in which case you would receive:

£ 7,324 a year if you are living at home,

£ 8,700 if you are living outside London and

£11,354 a year if you live away from home in London.

If your household income is more than £25,000 a year, the government expects your parents or guardians to contribute to your education, so only 45% to 50% of the loan is guaranteed, the rest being calculated on the basis of their income.

No matter what the cost of your course, the repayments would be the same; you pay nothing while you are studying. After that, if you get a job, you pay nothing until you earn £25,000 a year, after which you would pay 9% or £90 a year.

How Much Would My Parents Have To Pay?

If the loan amount is £8,700 a year, they would contribute nothing at all so long as the household income remains under £25,000.

Should it rise to £30,000, the loan amount would be £7,825 and they would pay £624.

At £40,000 the loan amount would be £6,828 and the parental payment £1,872.

At £50,000, the loan amount would be £5,579 with £3,121 to be paid by the parents.

At £60,000, they would pay £4,369 on a loan amount of £4,331.

That's Fine - But What About My Living Costs?

You can also take out a 'maintenance' loan which is paid once a term to cover such living costs as accommodation, food, books, socialising, laundry and travel.

Again, the maximum amount available is £8,700 a year, but how much you get depends on your family's gross household income and whether you are living at home or elsewhere.

The following chart shows the most you would get each week, although the amounts may change each year, depend-ing on the government's annual budget.

Repayment is calculated at the same rate as for the student loan - 9% or £90.

Place of Residence	Maximum amount per week
Living with Parents	£ 61
Away from home Outside London	£ 93
Away from home In London	£120
Living abroad	£129

Incidentally, all the figures quoted on student and maintenance loans may change as a result of government budgets, inflation and any resultant increase in the bank rate.

The figures may also differ in Scotland, Wales and Northern Ireland, although the differences are unlikely to be major.

Should I Pay Off My Student Loan Early?

You can - but although in general you should *always* pay a loan off as quickly as you can, with student loans it may not be a good idea.

That's because the repayments are based on your earnings, not how much you borrowed.

So, for example, if you never earn more than £25,000, the debt would be wiped after 30 years and you would not have to pay anything back.

In fact, if you earned less than £11,850, you wouldn't pay any tax either - not that I am suggesting you should deliberately earn as little as you can in order to avoid paying tax.

That's not exactly a great way to get rich!

Unfortunately, there is one other factor that we can do nothing about and that is the risk that the government will change the rules.

Politicians are not renowned for standing by past promises, so it is always possible that the £25,000 limit or the 30-year rule will be altered at some future date.

We simply don't know and will have to react accordingly at the time, if that does happen.

Is it worth going to University?

Given that approximately 62% of graduates never find graduate-worthy jobs and the debt that a student incurs by going to university, there is obviously a strong need to discuss very carefully indeed whether doing so is actually worth it.

In certain cases, there obviously is – especially if a student is studying the sciences.

Those students taking the arts and media lines might be advised to think very carefully indeed.

Ask whether you would be better off in the long term working even for a low salary and saving money that can be invested over time or amassing a debt that they may never be able to pay off.

What do I do if I'm in debt already?

If you are up a creek without a paddle, the only solution is to get to dry land as fast as you can and *make* yourself a paddle.

So it is with credit card debt. Getting out of it will not be easy and depending on how much you owe it could take several years. But all is not doom and gloom, as we shall see.

Even if you are in debt, you can still become a millionaire. All it needs is *self discipline!*

Here are some suggestions as to what you might do:

Say to yourself every morning: "I'm going to pay this off and I will never get into debt again". Repeat just before you go to bed. Persuade your mind that this *will* happen.

Repetition means that your sub-conscious mind will accept what you are telling it as fact, and act accordingly.

Be absolutely ruthless with yourself. Start by cutting up your credit card - or cards - and bin them so that you can't spend any more with them.

You can keep one bank debit card, which you can use anywhere, in order to pay for essentials. Do *not* use it to get cash. Use this *only* for essentials, not for treats. Pay off the full amount monthly.

Work out exactly how much income you receive and how much you spend each month. Then calculate how much you owe. If you go online, you can find free budget calculators to help you with this.

Look for savings wherever you can. Cut out the morning coffee at Costa, the chocolate bar, the crisps, the junk food. If you have a mobile phone, try to get a cheaper deal. Then shovel every pound, dollar or whatever into a savings account and use that to pay off your debt.

It may be good idea to move your credit card and get a '0% balance transfer card' deal. This means you can stop paying interest and start reducing the actual debt.

Be very careful because these deals incur fees. If you are consolidating debt on several credit cards onto one card, the fee can be very high.

There is a time limit on 0% balance transfer card deals, sometimes as long as three years. But you *must* pay off enough each month and clear the balance by the end of that period.

Otherwise you will just get into more debt. If you are in doubt, seek expert advice online. These websites may help:

https://www.gov.uk/options-for-paying-off-your-debts
Www.nationaldebtadvice.org/Debt/Help

In the United States, the National Foundation for Credit Counselling (www.nfcc.org) can be a great help. This is a non-profit organisation represented in all 50 states.

If you opt not to use a 0% Balance Transfer Card, pay off the cards with the highest rate of interest and the greatest amount of debt first.

Another option is to take out a personal loan to pay off all your credit card debts, so that you can then focus just on paying of the loan. If you do this, set up a Standing Order so that the payment is automatic.

Consider getting a second, part-time job, even if it only pays a few pounds an hour, and you work for only a couple of hours a week. It all helps.

Remember, every little saving, every payment is gradually reducing your overall debt and one day, you will no longer have it. When that happens, start saving every penny, cent, zloty or whatever that you can. You will then, finally, be on the road to *making* money, *growing* money and eventually achieving wealth.

So, What Have We Learnt So Far?

1. First, re-read the last two pages of Chapter One to remind yourself how to make a fortune.

2. Two Golden Rules: Never get into debt. And if you *do* get into debt, get out of it as fast as you can.

3. Compounding can work against you. Minimum payments are pure poison.

4. The misery of debt. Half the British population are at risk of being in debt for the rest of their lives. Don't be one of them!

5. Avoid 'special offers'. You gain nothing in the long run. The benefits go to the advertising companies.

6. Banks and credit card companies benefit from your being in debt. That's why they have 'fat cat' salaries of hundreds of thousands and often millions of pounds a year.

7. How we are gradually becoming cashless societies - and how that means you spend more on credit and debit cards and thus lose control of your money.

8. The importance of using a Spending App to keep a check on your income and how much you spend.

9. Why you should not be fearful of student loans.

10. How to go about paying off your credit card debt if you have read this book too late.

11. Not to despair. There are millions of other people in the same boat. You are ahead of the game because you now know the possibilities and challenges ahead.

-£££-

Chapter Three

SURVIVING THE FINANCIAL MINEFIELD

In every field of life, there are dangers and the financial world is no exception.

There are all kinds of pitfalls which you need to avoid at all costs - and 'costs' is the operative word here.

Therefore, it's important to prepare yourself so that you will be able to recognize the pitfalls when they pop up unexpectedly.

As we have seen, there are countless people out there who will try to persuade you to buy *their* product by pretending that *you* will benefit, whereas the truth is that they are more interested in boosting their own wealth with *your* money.

Then there is this guy called Murphy. Murphy's Law states that: 'If it can go wrong, it will go wrong' - and unfortunately Murphy all too often is right.

All kinds of things can go wrong - like selling or buying into stocks and shares at the wrong time, buying investment funds that don't live up to their promise, or falling for some 'Get Rich Quick' scheme that actually makes you poorer.

A Close Shave

So, stay with me and I will guide you through this minefield - and believe me, I know a thing or two about minefields!

When I was an on-screen television reporter for ITN's *News at Ten,* I was assigned to go to West Beirut, where fighters of the Palestinian Liberation Organisation were under siege by the Israeli armed forces.

My assignment was to be one of the first journalists to get into West Beirut and find out what it was like to be bombed and shelled by land, sea and air for as much as 17 hours a day.

It wasn't exactly a bundle of fun, especially as one day I was walking with my cameraman Mickey Inglis, soundman John Soldini and producer Mike Nolan across some waste ground with 500 pound bombs falling all around us when Micky suddenly exclaimed:

"Hang on a minute - it's mined."

We all froze. Our nerves suddenly jumped about two inches off our skin. Then John Soldini, who was just behind me, muttered: "They didn't put this in the brochure, Sam."

That broke the tension and, gingerly, we retreated the same way that we had come. It had been a very close shave!

What to Watch Out For!

The financial minefield is no different. There are all kinds of special offers, schemes, traps and hidden costs out there - and you need to know about them because, if you are not careful, they can put a very large spoke in your future wheel of fortune.

Consequently, it is vital that you how it all works. For those of you in the 14-18 age bracket who are just beginning to show an interest in money matters, that calls for a few definitions, so that we all know what we are talking about.

I know this is a bit boring, but stick with it because unless someone leaves you a pot of money, you can *only* get rich by investing your money in businesses around the world.

To do that, you really do need to understand the nitty gritty of the financial sector. Once you do, you will have entered a very exciting world!

Stocks and Shares

Like most things, companies have a value which depends on how successful the company is. If a company is registered on the Stock Exchange, an investor can buy or sell a share of that company.

When you buy several shares, they are called stocks. Stocks represent a claim on the company's profits and assets (i.e. what the company owns, such as property).

The more stock you buy, the greater your share of the ownership, so if you buy enough shares to reach 50% ownership, you obviously have a commanding say in how the company is run.

Once you own shares, a company will pay you a dividend - which is to say a proportionate percentage of the company profits.

You can then either take the annual dividend as income or you can re-invest it, adding it to the overall value of your investment account.

Of course, the value of companies can go up - or down, depending, for example, on how much the company exports to other countries or how much the managers have had to borrow to invest in more staff, specific projects and so on.

Obviously, as the value of a company rises or falls, so do the shares - sometimes quite quickly.

If a company is seen to be running into problems, the price of its stock could drop like the 70-ton Boeing I mentioned earlier.

When the stock market (the exchange where you buy your shares) is driven by the fear of rising inflation, a decline in the housing market, exports or other indicators, investors might well decide to sell the shares (driving the market even further down) and instead buy bonds.

Bonds

Bonds are essentially promises by a government or corporate company to pay a *fixed* rate of interest on a specific date in the future to investors who lend them money, no matter what the market or the country's economy is doing.

In other words they are an I.O.U.

So, for example, if a government or company wants to raise money in order to build a road, railway, hospital, a dam or some other major project, they will offer a bond.

You may wish to invest in that bond by lending them part of the money required.

Why would you do this? Because whereas the price of shares can be volatile (i.e. gain or lose very quickly), bonds are much steadier.

The gain may not be as much as for a share, but the bond is a safer, more cautious investment.

That's because the price of bonds are bound by interest rates, not by profitability.

If a company goes bankrupt, investors who hold bonds are repaid in full from the liquidation of the company before shareholders are paid anything

What all this means is that bonds are less risky than shares, although they don't offer the potentially fast gains that you can get with stocks and shares.

Mutual Funds

A mutual fund is created by a company whose manager and expert analysts check every last detail of a variety of companies and then buy the stocks, bonds and other assets they believe have the greatest potential to make money.

The money to buy the portfolio of stocks, bonds and other is ultimately provided by you, the investor.

The manager and his analysts specialize in specific types of companies across a wide assortment of business sectors - such as chemical, retail, banking, oil, automotive and so on.

So by investing in a mutual fund, you are pooling your money with other investors.

Instead of doing your own research into specific companies and buying individual shares of your own choosing, you are spreading your money across a variety of investments chosen by the manager and analysts, and thus minimizing your risk.

Active Management

Mutual funds are either passively or actively managed. In the latter, the manager frequently buys and sells the stocks, bonds and other assets in his bid to increase the fund's gains - and consequently boost his own reputation.

For his knowledge and efforts, you pay a fee of between one and perhaps as much as four or even five per cent of your profits.

Index Tracker Funds

An index fund is essentially a list of stocks or bonds. For example, the Dow Jones Industrial Average is a list of 30 'blue chip' stocks - 'blue chip' meaning very large companies with a huge amount of capital (cash and other holdings).

Similarly, the FTSE 100 is a list of the top 100 companies in the United Kingdom. There is also an index of the FTSE 250 top companies as well as the FTSE all share index.

The S&P 500 (Standard & Poor's) index comprises the 500 American companies with the most capital and thus the most valuable.

In other words, an index tracking fund is pretty much the same as a mutual fund. The difference is that if you invest in an index tracking fund, you are investing in a share of *all* the stocks or bonds listed in that fund, rather than in a much smaller portfolio of selected assets chosen by managers and analysts.

So, when investing you can choose:

(a) Whether to study every detail of companies yourself and then invest in the companies *you* believe will succeed,

(b) To invest in a mutual fund which will charge you a percentage of your profits to pay for the manager, analysts and transaction fees, or

(c) Invest in an index tracker fund for which the charges are very low and in some cases almost negligible, which is to say always below one per cent and usually less than 0.25%.

If you invest in the S&P 500, Vanguard 500, FTSE 100 or 250 or FTSE All Share Indexes, you would be buying into some of the most successful companies in the world for a negligible fee - companies that have survived recessions, depressions, all kinds of negative influences and even wars.

And you wouldn't have to research and choose stocks yourself or pay a fund manager to help you. All that has already been done for you.

The fact is that buying into an actively managed mutual fund is not only hugely expensive, it's also a leap of blind faith because, basically, you are hoping that the fund manager is better at picking stocks than your are.

If you do your own research into companies, you *might* be lucky and discover one or two companies that are greatly under-valued and have enormous potential.

Then again, you might not.

Fund Managers Follow Their Emotions, Too!

Fund managers and analysts, naturally, have a better chance of success than you do because they spend their entire working days searching for these great opportunities.

But they are only human and in the great chase to beat the next guy, they, too, let their emotions run away with them, buying when excitement about a rising market is at its highest - and selling when the market falls and everything is going pear-shaped.

It's one of the reasons why, so few actively managed mutual funds are able to beat the gains achieved by the overall market over longer period of time. Makes you think, doesn't it?

Other Funds - But Not for Now!

There are several other types of funds - Money Market Funds, Hedge Funds and the like, but we don't need to bother about those here.

Hedge funds are an investment partnership between a professional fund manager and investors who pool their money into the fund, the aim of which is to maximize profits and eliminate the risk.

In some respects, they are similar to mutual funds but they tend to be very aggressive, risky and exclusive. Hedge fund managers frequently require a *minimum* initial investment of one million pounds as an entrance fee!

So, no need to worry about those just yet - although you may well be interested in them in the future!

Learning the Rules.

Tens of millions of people invest in mutual funds, but in my view they are signing up to a pretty rotten deal.

Let's say they invest £1,000. They would have to pay as much as 40%, perhaps even more, of their profits to pay the costs of the fund manager and analysts who decide which companies or institutions in which to invest your money.

Worse still, if they invest it in companies or other funds that actually *lose* money, you are the one who has to accept that loss. They still get paid - by you!

Yet despite this, hundreds of millions of people around the world have invested a mind-boggling $12.2 *trillion* dollars in the mutual fund industry.

It's crazy. Why? Because those people are paying horrendous amounts of money for the privilege of investing in what is also known as an 'actively managed' fund.

Uncovering the Truth

Hidden fees and taxes can eat into your investments like a plague of locusts in a field of barley.

Worse, the negative compounding effect can have a significant effect even if the various fees are relatively small.

If, for example, you invested £1,000 and gained 6% interest over 10 years, you would have £1,791.

However, if your management and other fees were 2% a year, you would end up paying £917.86, or more than half your pot of gold in fees, leaving you with only £873.14.

That's less than your original investment and less than half the profit you would have made if you had had no fees to pay.

Imagine if in later life you had £100,000 invested at the same interest rates over the same ten years. You would then be looking at a whopping £91,786 paid in fees.

Ideally, you should be paying no more than an *absolute* maximum of 1.25% in fees.

That should include the ongoing cost of the investment as well as for a financial investment advisor to help you buy the right funds and re-adjust the balance of your portfolio from time to time.

How Fees Eat Your Profits

Year	6% Growth with no fee	6% growth minus 2%	Minus 2% fees	Actual growth
Year 1	£1,068	-	-£20.76	£1,047.24
Year 2	£1,124	£1,047.24	-£20.94	£1,026.30
Year 3	£1,191	£1,026.30	-£20.53	£1,005.77
Year 4	£1,262	£1,005.77	-£20.12	£ 985.65
Year 5	£1,338	£ 985.65	-£19.71	£ 965.94
Year 6	£1,419	£ 965.94	-£19.32	£ 946.62
Year 7	£1,504	£ 946.62	-£18.93	£ 927.69
Year 8	£1,594	£ 927.69	-£18.55	£909.14
Year 9	£1,689	£ 909.14	-£18.18	£ 890.96
Year 10	**£1,791**	£ 890.96	-£17.82	**£ 873.14**

The Colossal Cost of Transaction Fees

On top of the 2% management and other fees, you're also charged for every transaction - in other words every time the manager decides to buy, sell or switch from one asset to another.

The fund manager's job is 'actively' to try and beat the market. In other words, by being better at choosing stocks and bonds than any other manager.

Given that there are tens of thousands, if not hundreds of thousands or, who knows, even millions of them, that's a tall order.

To keep ahead of the game, a fund manager has to 'actively' change the assets in his fund on a regular basis, following up on hot tips and the latest ratings by companies like Morningstar, a Chicago based investment research firm.

Fund managers are not just flogging off a handful of shares or bonds. They are manipulating their portfolios - and your money - to a huge extent.

In other words, if they were managing a fund of £10 million of stocks, they could well be buying and selling as much as £8 million of those stocks each year.

Can you imagine the overall cost of that when you add in the broker's commission, a broker being the middle man in the sale?

Not to mention the bid-ask spread, which is to say the difference between the selling price and the buying price.

Needless to say, you have to pay more to buy and get less when you sell.

Added together, all these extra costs are huge - and you would be the mug that's paying for it all.

And As If That's Not Enough...

Of course, you are not only paying ongoing fees and transaction fees. There are many additional costs that you don't even realise you are paying.

There may be entry and exit fees. You may be

charged for the privilege of being able to review your whole portfolio at any time and use various tools to help you figure out which investments to buy and which to avoid. That could add another 0.25% to the cost.

Some actively managed funds also charge performance fees - so you would pay a higher fee if the fund succeeds in beating a given target.

Need the help of a financial advisor? That, too, incurs charges - and believe me, there are plenty of advisors to help. But like fund managers, the majority of them are no better at picking stocks than the next advisor.

Fund managers also have to 'sell' their funds and persuade punters to invest in their particular fund rather than someone else's. So, there's also advertising to pay for! And guess who will be paying for it!

And One More Con!

I've spent some 50 years as a journalist and all journalists will tell you that statistics are their best friend. You can do anything with them. I think it was Mark Twain who said: "Lies, lies and statistics".

If you tell me that a piece of cloth is 80% cotton, I can tell you that 20% of it polyester.

If four people each stand on a corner of a crossroads and witness an accident, the police will tell you that they will hear four different versions of what happened.

In other words, you can't really believe anything that you read in the financial minefield.

When a fund manager reports that a mutual fund returned, say, a ten per cent gain, that is - to put it kindly - a manipulated figure.

The fact is that you, the investor, will actually receive considerably less. In other words, it's a con!

Like so many hidden costs, the details are masked in complicated gobbledygook such as the difference between *time-weighted* returns and *dollar-weighted* returns, which can reduce your return till further.

You Don't Need To Know What These Mean!

You need only be aware that it is one more way to fool you into buying into a fund that won't give you the return the manager says it will.

It was John Bogle, another of the world's greatest investors and founder of the Vanguard Group of Funds, who first exposed this devious trickery.

Over one 25 year period, Bogle noted that the average mutual fund earned a return of 7.8 per cent. That was 1.3% less than the 9.1% of the S&P 500 index.

Oddly, though, the average fund investor didn't even earn that much.

To work out what the *investor* earned, you have to consider the transactions - the movement of money into and out of the fund.

Money flows *into* a fund mostly after a fund has performed well. Conversely, it flows *out* after a poor performance.

When you take all this into account, you find that the investor did *not* earn the 7.8% reported by the fund manager. Instead, his return amounted to only 6.3%. That's 2.3% less than the S&P 500 index.

As they say, every little helps - the fund manager, that is. Not you!

It Didn't Used To Be Like That!

Fifty years ago, life was much simpler. You went to a stock broker, who would recommend various companies which had promise and were predicted to be successful, and you would buy their shares and then wait for years, hopefully to see a profit.

Since then, hidden costs have gradually permeated the mutual fund industry. Mutual fund 'wizards' have managed to shroud these in jargon - soft dollar costs, cash drag costs and the like, making them difficult to understand and, as a consequence, effectively brushing them under the carpet.

Some years ago, Forbes Magazine published an article listing the *true* costs of mutual funds. In a non-taxable account, those costs totalled up to 3.17% - and 4.17% on a taxable account.

Not worth bothering about? You have to be kidding!

Quite aside from these hidden costs, you will also have to pay taxes on any holdings unless your funds are in an ISA (Individual Savings Account) in Britain or an IRA or Roth IRA in the United States.

These are funds in which you can hold dividends, interest and capital gains free of tax. As we have seen, in Britain, you are allowed to put a maximum £20,000 of assets a year into an ISA.

Otherwise, the taxman nails you to the wall.

So How Well Do Actively Managed Funds Do?

Not very! Despite all these hidden costs less than five per cent of actively managed funds actually match or beat the market. That's a pathetic performance.

Apart from this very small percentage of fund managers, it's hard to find a financial analyst or fund manager out there who can pick stocks and funds any better than anyone else.

One more Profit Gobbler

As if fees, advertising, high manager and analyst salaries, not to mention the devious manipulation of statistics, inflation and a crazy race to buy the latest 'hot' stocks, were not enough, there's one more profit gobbler to consider.

Taxation!

We've seen how you can protect your honey pot from taxation by investing in ISAs, IRAs and Roth IRAs each year, and it is wise to invest to the legal limit in them.

Unfortunately, most mutual funds are not tax-efficient, not least because of the fund managers' frenzied quest to trade the stocks in their portfolios.

As a result, in the 20 years from the end of the Second World War, the average turnover of mutual funds was only about 15-16% and fund managers would hold their stocks for five or six years.

Long-term Investment Or Short-Term Speculation?

Today, it seems as if fund managers today prefer short-term speculation to long term investment - and that is the road to potential disaster.

Thanks to feverish trading and a high portfolio turnover, the resultant annual taxation can amount to some 15% of the total pre-tax return.

That's one big hole in your profits!

And Finally, Inflation!

There seem to be so many aspects designed to stop us earning our fortune.

We've had dodgy 'Get Rich Quick Schemes', ongoing fees, transaction costs, soft-dollar costs, cash drag, redemption fees, exchange fees, account fees, purchase fees, entry and exit fees, and 'bla bla bla' fees.

Not to mention hectic trading and taxation - and that's not all because we haven't mentioned one final barrier: inflation combined with the effects of currency markets, national economies and such financial devices as quantitative easing.

That's a fancy way of saying 'printing money' to survive an economic downturn. It may help for a while, but in the end it simply devalues the amount of your currency.

Inflation, which does the same thing, is arguably the most greedy locust of the lot.

If the supply of money outpaces economic growth it will result in increased prices for goods and services - and that means that the purchasing power decreases.

In short, inflation means that everything you buy effectively costs more because your currency, your savings and your investments aren't worth as much.

How Money Becomes Less Valuable

The British pound, for example, is one of the oldest reserve currencies in the world, but between 1975 and 1976 high unemployment and inflation forced the government to beg for a loan from the International Monetary Fund.

Similarly, in 1967 the pound was worth US$2.50. These days, it is worth around US$1.30.

Not that the dollar has fared any better. In 1913, the Federal Reserve - actually a privately-owned central bank, took over the U.S. banking system.

Since then, the value of the dollar has fallen steadily, losing a massive 96% of its value. To put that into context, the dollar today would be worth only about three cents back in 1913.

The reason for this decline is that the Federal Reserve has been printing money as if there was no tomorrow. Quantitative easing may mean more dollars in circulation, but more paper money also means the value is less.

All this does is to create inflation. So, you can imagine that if the Federal Reserve hadn't tampered with the dollar's value, how much more valuable investors' money would be today.

Where There Are Mega-Bucks, There Are Sharks

The world of finance is like an ocean full of sharks. It is both sad and cynical to have to say that there are liars, cheats and con artists at every turn, and that you can't really trust anyone.

Even banks and some of the largest and best known investment companies are run by people who in some cases are dishonest and in others more interested in making their own fortunes than anything else. You only have to look at the monstrous salaries of Chief Executives to see that.

The problem is that the finance world is awash with billions of dollars and there are plenty of fraudsters out there willing to take any chance to get their grubby hands on them.

Scandals That Rocked The World

In the past decade there have been all too many scandals. For example, the Texas-based energy company, Enron, which secretly ran into millions of dollars of debt.

For six consecutive years, Forbes Magazine described it as the most innovative company in the United States - until without warning, it's share price dropped like a stone and the company went bankrupt.

A year later, Worldcom's boss, Bernard Ebbers, was sentenced to 25 years in jail after more than $7 *billion* 'accounting errors' were discovered.

Bernard Madoff, the head of his own investment company in Wall Street was another financial crook. He was a fraudster *par excellence*, swindling investors of nearly $65 billion.

Well, the American justice system knows how to deal with people like Mr. Madoff. He was sentenced to 150 years in jail!

In the 2008 financial crisis, Lehman Brothers, a financial services company more than 150 years old and the fourth largest investment bank in America, went bust thanks to what's known as 'cosmetic accounting'. That's a euphemism for cheating.

Then there was Libor, a global interest rate 20 times the size of the U.S. economy. Libor affected some $350 *trillion* of assets worldwide and was used by banks and financial institutions all over the world.

Then it was discovered that the rate was being fixed illegally by banks over or under reporting the rate.

If they raised the rate by just a few points, the banks (which is to say bank managers, traders and employees) could make truck loads of cash - several hundred million in a couple of minutes.

That little scam cost American government institutions some $6 billion.

So Who Can You Trust?

The misappropriation of client funds, insider trading convictions, bank traders rigging the rates and so on don't make for a safe financial environment.

Consequently, it is important to take lessons from these scandals and always to do your homework when investing.

Don't ever take anything for granted.

But as Julian of Norwich said: "All will be well. All manner of things will be well" and I will show you how to invest safely and wisely, and how to keep it really simple so that you don't have to worry about all these scams.

In whatever field, there are ups and downs in life and the financial world is no different. Companies collapse. Banks collapse. Stock markets crash.

But life is cyclical. What goes up must eventually come down - and vice versa. As the Chinese would say: "When life is really bad, that is the time to be happy."

So there is no need to panic and throw in the towel. Relax. Follow the advice in this little book and you can ignore it all, because in 30, 40, 50 or even 60 years, your investments will ultimately average out -- and you will be wealthy without worrying.

There was a saying in Wall Street that 'Greed is Good'. I suggest that 'Average is Better!'

An Apology - And a Suggestion!

There we are. If you have read to this point, you may well feel a little depressed. If you do, I apologise.

However, it is necessary because if you don't know the pitfalls, you can't avoid falling headlong into them.

So now, may I suggest you re-read Chapter One? Just to boost your spirits and remind yourself about the magic of compounding.

And if it is any comfort, by reading this far, you are well on your way to understanding *how* to make money without really trying.

What Have We Learned in this Chapter?

1. To watch out for and avoid dodgy 'Get Rick Quick' schemes and special offers.

2. The meaning of stocks, shares, bonds, Mutual Funds, active management and Index Tracker Funds.

3. The truth about fees and how they eat away at

your profits.

4. The astronomical cost of transaction and other fees.

5. To be aware of all the other hidden costs and how fund managers make light of them

6. How actively managed mutual funds are not all they are cracked up to be.

7. The effects of taxation and the frenzied trading of fund managers.

8. The effects of inflation and devaluation of currencies.

9. Not to become depressed by the potential setbacks to earning money.

10. To concentrate instead on the Miracle of Compounding and how you *can* make your fortune over time despite the pitfalls with patience, discipline and the careful allocation of your funds.

-£££-

Chapter Four

FROM HEALTH TO WEALTH

If you have read this far, you have already proved that you really do want to be wealthy.

As I wrote in the introduction, you *can* achieve this simply by following the initial eight steps listed on the first couple of pages of this book.

Nevertheless, you will be infinitely more successful if you follow the strategy in this chapter, first learning how your physical health and fitness will automatically lead to a healthy and more *positive* mindset.

This in turn will help you to focus your mind on the goals ahead and equip you to the greatest possible degree when it come to learning more about the financial world, how it works and what you need to know about investing to avoid the pitfalls.

Making a fortune can take time. It demands patience - maybe 30, 40 or 50 years of patience.

But take heart!

When you think positively and focus resolutely on the task ahead, you will find that you will make money faster than you could ever imagine.

As a first step, it is a huge help if you know *why* you want to be rich. Do you want to be a millionaire, a multi-millionaire or just wealthy enough not to have to worry about money?

What do you want the money *for?* Is it for the possessions that money can buy? Or is it for something more profound?

Why not start by making a list. Lists help you to focus on *exactly* what it is that you desire. For example:

MY MISSION AND MY DREAM

1. To be a millionaire by the time I am 30 years old.
2. To own a Ferrari, Aston Martin or Lamborghini.
3. To travel first class wherever I go.
4. To stay in the best hotels and eat in the best restaurants in the world.
5. To travel to exotic locations whenever I wish.
6. To know that I have enough money to pay all the bills without worrying.
7. To educate my children and have enough money for a comfortable retirement.

Money Isn't Everything - But It Helps!

When you begin to ask yourself what it is that *really* drives your desire for wealth, the answer is not so much 'things', as listed above but gut feelings.

Probably the most important of these is security. The knowledge that no matter what happens in life, you will be comfortable and don't have to worry about money.

Of course, you want everything on the list above. But you may also be driven by the challenge of achieving it, by the excitement of watching your humble beginnings grow and eventually achieve those goals.

Later, as you become wealthy, you will probably find joy in *sharing* your wealth and helping others achieve their goals.

Last night, (before writing these words), I was watching a television documentary with my wife about wildlife in Puerto Rico.

This is a beautiful Caribbean island which once was 90% covered with forest. But a fast-growing population has reduced the forest to about 54% and in the last five years hurricanes have destroyed as many as 30 million trees.

That has placed several species of animal, birds and mammals in danger of extinction. The programme showed how a handful of dedicated Puerto Ricans have been battling for years - in one instance several decades - to save the now endangered Puerto Rican Parrot.

They are also helping to save the coqui frog, a tiny creature the size of a thumbnail that has become a national symbol, and a strange sea mammal called a manatee.

These volunteers have worked so hard, giving their spare time and asking nothing in return.

Their reward was knowing that by catching a few parrots and helping them to breed, they have been able to release 43 pairs of birds into the wild, having trained them to look after themselves after several years in captivity.

Other volunteers probably saved the life of a rare manatee which had a poisonous infection requiring a surgical operation.

Immediately after the programme, I was consumed with a desire to help these people and others like them, and wrote a memorandum to myself that when - like you - I have become wealthy, I will do so because they are so worth it!

Indeed, I believe fervently that the desire to give and share your wealth is an essential part of *becoming* wealthy.

And that brings me to the Law of Attraction.

The Law of Attraction

If you want to make money, you have to *think* money. You have to persuade your sub-conscious mind that:

1. you have the mental capacity to stick with your beliefs through thick and thin, and

2. that you truly *believe,* deep down in your bones,

that you *will* achieve the riches you desire.

That's where the Law of Attraction comes in. In essence, this is a law that is said to enable every human being, irrespective of nationality, sex, colour, creed, religious belief or financial circumstances, to achieve whatever they want if they want it enough.

It is the belief that if you say to yourself every day that *anything - everything - is possible*, that belief will eventually permeate your sub-conscious mind and those thoughts will then translate into reality.

In other words, if you *think* about being a millionaire at every opportunity throughout the day, the Law of Attraction helps to ensure that it happens

Be Specific About Your Dreams

In order to convince your sub-conscious mind that you are serious about achieving wealth, you need to be specific about your goals.

Why do you want to be rich? *How* rich? And *when?*

Unless your sub-conscious mind knows the answer to these questions, neither it nor the Law of Attraction with which it is in harmony can help you.

So make a list. Is it because you want a Ferrari or Lamborghini in the garage? Because you want to impress people? Live in a fine house with a sea view and a swimming pool?

Close your eyes and *picture* yourself in that house by the sea. Imagine yourself *driving* your Lamborghini, *visualize* yourself walking into an expensive suite at a famous hotel or relaxing in the top suite of a luxury cruise ship.

That may seem a bit whacky but, believe me, it is the first and perhaps an essential step to creating your winning financial strategy.

Beware of Nay-Sayers and Negative Thinkers

Of course, there will always be people that rubbish this idea, who will tell you that the Law of Attraction is ridiculous, that it can't work, that there's no proof that it even exists.

They may be right. But supposing they are not?

The Law of Attraction belongs in the world of quantum physics and you and I know very little about that world because even leading physicists and scientists are only just beginning to understand it.

So why throw away the chance that it *might* exist, that it can be an enormous help to you and that they may be wrong?

It's the same argument as climate change. Some people deny that it is happening and continue to use plastic bags and aerosols and all the rest.

Others say: 'Okay, even if we don't know for sure' why screw up the planet for our children and grandchildren. Let's clean up the planet - just in case it's true."

Whatever people say about the Law of Attraction, I certainly believe - and know from previous experience - that it does work.

I know because at one stage of my life, I was homeless.

A Sorry Tale

I had been working in Sweden and, sadly, my marriage had broken up. Devastated, I decided to move to London and managed to get a job at the BBC World Service.

However, as I was not a member of the Journalists' Union at the time, I was employed only on a day-to-day, no contract basis.

So when a national newspaper, the Daily Sketch, folded, scores of journalists who were members of the union suddenly found themselves out of a job.

The BBC, of course, was committed to taking some of them on and the next thing I knew was that I, too, was out of a job.

Unfortunately, I had only about £500 in the bank and after a few weeks, I was no longer able to pay the rent on the room in which I was living in Craven Terrace in Paddington.

The upshot of all this was that I ended up spending my nights on a bench on Platform One at Paddington Station in London.

Homelessness strikes immediately. Suddenly, you have nowhere to put your clothes. You can't iron your shirts and, worse, it is difficult to shave. I had to do so in the Paddington Station washrooms where in those days there was no soap and only cold water.

Worse, when you have to sleep in your clothes, they quickly become crumpled and that is not the best way to go to an interview.

I walked all over London searching for a job. Each time, I walked out of interviews having been told: "We'll keep your name and details on file." Over and over again.

Yet throughout this time, I never lost faith in my ability as a journalist and I *knew* instinctively that all would be well in the end.

So, for all the discomforts, I was happy. I was free!

Saved By An American. Crying!

To feed myself, I would saunter round a small café on the station. Here, people waiting for trains would have a cup of tea and a sandwich, a pork pie or an Eccles cake and occasionally a piece of cake.

When their train came in, they would often dash off,

leaving part of their food behind. That's when I swooped in, helping myself.

One day, a Friday, I saw a man sitting there, crying. I asked him what was the matter. He brushed me off with a wave of his hand, but I persisted.

Somehow, I felt that *I* could help *him*.

"Come on, tell me," I said.

He looked up and muttered that his wife had left him.

"I'm sorry. I know how you must feel," I said, adding that the same thing had happened to me a few months earlier.

He perked up a bit then and was interested to know my story.

When I told him I was a journalist and had been the Chief Scandinavian Correspondent for Reuters News Agency and more recently had worked for Swedish Radio and the BBC World Service, he said:

"I don't believe it. That's amazing!"

He introduced himself as Paul Shay and went on to explain that he was the Editor of a new magazine to be published in a month's time.

He asked about my circumstances. Why was I scrounging food that people had left on their tables? How did I end up homeless?

Clearly the belief that I had in myself, the way that I spoke and my positive attitude impressed him. He suggested that I come to see him at his office the following Monday.

I did and for 13 months I worked as his Chief News Editor. Once again, I was able to rent a room in Paddington.

Sadly, the magazine folded due to a lack of advertising. We were informed by the owner - again on a Friday - that as of five o'clock that evening we would be unemployed.

By an incredible coincidence, though, when I arrived back at my room there was a letter on my doorstep. It was from Visnews, the television arm of Reuters News Agency offering me a job as a scriptwriter.

I couldn't explain it, but it was as if my positive and cheerful mindset had attracted a solution at exactly the right time.

And it wasn't the only time that happened.

Learning The Tools of a New Trade

Visnews was effectively an agency buying film from around the world, editing it into short news items with a commentary and selling these on to television stations around the world.

We received tens of thousands of feet of film a week and after the footage had been edited, my job was to write a script for the narrator.

Other more senior scriptwriters taught me how best to do that, making sure that the subject of a sentence was also the subject of the shots in the film.

Eventually, I became a reporter covering stories from Belfast during the 'Troubles' of the 1970s.

That was when members of the IRA and various Protestant organisations went around murdering each other and blowing up entire streets both in Northern Ireland and mainland Britain.

Then, in December 1972, by which time I had joined the National Union of Journalists, I spotted an advertisement for a scriptwriter at ITN, working on all ITN's national news bulletins, including *News at Ten.*

I applied immediately. There was not a shadow of doubt in my mind that I would get the job. So far as I was concerned, that advertisement was directed specifically at me.

Visualising Success

Just before the interview, I glimpsed the newsroom and in my mind pictured myself sitting at a desk there. I even imagined standing in front of a camera, reporting the latest developments of a news story.

I just *knew* the job was mine. At the interview, I think I asked more questions than the man interviewing me (David Nicholas, later Sir David Nicholas, the Editor of ITN).

A week or so later, an envelope with the ITN logo dropped onto my doormat.

I joined ITN on January 3rd, 1973, eventually rising from the status of scriptwriter to 'fixer' (a kind of field producer) and ultimately to a reporter and occasional news presenter.

Someone once said that "You are what you think." If anything was proof that the Law of Attraction, a positive mindset and visualisation can help you to attain success, surely this story was it.

Strange How Coincidences Occur

Has anybody ever mentioned to you some exotic holiday destination within easy reach? A place that makes you curious and excited?

Have you then noticed that suddenly there is an article in a magazine about it? Or that by pure chance you meet someone who has just been there?

That is how the Law of Attraction works. Your mind becomes attuned to this exotic place - and the next thing you know all kinds of coincidences relating to it occur.

Perhaps by chance you spot a video about it on YouTube - a video you probably wouldn't have noticed or shown any interest in previously.

When you tell yourself repeatedly that you are going to be very wealthy, your sub-conscious mind will accept that as a *certainty.*

It will then act as a magnet to attract in some mysterious way all the elements that will transform that certainty into *reality.*

Transforming Thoughts into Reality

The Law of Attraction is an extremely well known concept and it's one of life's great mysteries.

People have spoken and written about it for centuries. Some say it all began with The Buddha.

When Buddhism reached the western world, we learned about 'karma'.

Buddhists believe human beings absorb good and bad karma throughout their current lives and then carry it with them indefinitely into future lives in whatever form those lives may take.

This is said to continue in a never-ending cycle of life and death until they reach a state of perfection known as 'Nirvana'.

Many of the world leaders in politics, science, finance, theatre, movies, art and other walks of life have adopted this philosophy.

Hundreds of thousands, if not millions, of people attribute their success to the Law of Attraction which, incidentally, has nearly six *million* fans on Facebook.

They believe that you can *control* your mind by repeatedly feeding into it the specific goals and dreams you wish to achieve in a given period of time..

If you *believe* that the mind then acts as a magnet to attract successful steps towards reaching those goals (i.e. financial success), then is there any good reason why it *wouldn't* work for you?

When you convince yourself that you will be

wealthy and commit yourself 1,000% to that aim, I have
no doubt at all that you - and I - will reach that goal.

The Smile You Give Out Returns To You

By insinuation, the Law of Attraction suggests that
when you give to charity and share your growing wealth
with others, the act of giving will also result in the act of
receiving.

It is the attraction of opposites that makes
magnetism what it is. Giving and receiving.

There is an Indian saying: "The Smile You Give Out
Returns To You!

Actually, that is not always true because there are in
this world some exceptionally grumpy people who
actually enjoy being miserable.

Ignore them.

There is no room in your life for negative thinking
people. Concentrate on the positives of life.

Associate with people like yourself - people who
also believe you can achieve anything in life because, in
the words of Les Brown, the motivational speaker I
mentioned earlier, it's *possible.* And it's worth it!

Creating Your Own Luck

Positive people who associate with other positive
people create their own luck.

When I was a television reporter for *News at Ten,*
the camera crew and I would often sit on a bed late at
night and discuss how we would treat the story the
following day.

By the time we had gone to bed, I had suggested
how we might approach the story and what ingredients we
would need.

The camera operator came up with suggestions
about how best we could achieve that plan. The sound

technician suggested that he might be able to use a radio microphone over one of the camera operator's shots. And so on.

The upshot was that when we set out, sometimes as early as five o'clock in the morning, we were a close-knit team.

Each one of us knew what we were looking for and how best to get it. In other words, we were creating our own luck.

A Yacht Sailing Before The Wind

To do that you also need to be flexible, taking the rough with the smooth. You need to be as fluid as water that you can move with your little finger but which can wear away the hardest stone.

Life can work for you or against you. You can be certain that it will do both.

There will be times when you make superb progress and others when you think your are up against a brick wall.

The journey towards achieving wealth is not unlike a yacht sailing before the wind.

In order to reach the harbour ahead of it, the yacht's crew must tack first to port, then to starboard, zigzagging across the ocean until finally, they reach port.

It may be rough at times. It may take time. But in the end, they get there. So the lesson here is to create a strategy.

Be clear in your own mind what it is *exactly* that you want.

Write down a list of these things and read it every morning. Think not so much about what you *want,* but what life will be like when you have achieved these goals.

How To Convince Yourself

Close your eyes for a few minutes every morning and *visualize* what your life will be like when you have wealth.

For example, say to yourself:

"When I am a millionaire, I will have a life without financial worry".

"I will travel first class, stay in five star hotels and eat in the best restaurants whenever I please."

"At the same time, I will also give to charity and help other people.

"People will respect me for doing that".

"I *love* money because it will ensure that I and my family live well."

Can't We Get On With It?

At this stage, you may well be wondering what all this has to do with the actual means of accumulating wealth, such as the nitty gritty of where to invest, what to invest in and why, and what is the best way to balance a portfolio.

In fact, you may well even be wondering what I mean by balancing a portfolio.

As I said, you do need patience! You will begin to learn the ins and outs of investing in Chapter Five and when you have finished this book, you will have the answer to all those questions.

So, please, don't be tempted to skip the rest of this chapter. It's very important! In fact, it is the *foundation* upon which you will build your entire future.

Good Health - A Vital First Step to Success

If Step One in the creation of your wealth strategy is

to convince yourself that all your goals are achievable (because they are *possible*), then Step Two is to have a healthy body.

This will automatically result in a healthy and positive mindset, greater self-esteem and lead to the utmost faith in yourself and your abilities.

Just as you must rid yourself of debt in order to create wealth, so if you are overweight you must lose pounds in order to have a healthy body and mind.

The Law of Attraction is a valuable tool here, too. But it is no good saying to yourself: "I'm going to be fit and healthy one day".

The Law of Attraction needs you to be specific and realistic. It needs an achievable goal,.

So, instead, write down and affirm to yourself: "I will lose two pounds a week until I reach my target weight of x" or "By the end of the year, I will be walking or jogging x miles a day, x times a week".

It's important to write down these affirmations and to picture yourself actually doing them in your mind.

Say 'YUK' to the Five CCCCCs

One way of visualizing your goals is to hang a notice board in a prominent place and cover it with newspaper clippings, pictures from magazines and perhaps cartoons - anything relating to your targets.

Photographs of healthy food, cyclists, joggers, hikers, headlines about the dangers of obesity and pictures of Big Macs and KFC meal deals crossed out in red and marked 'YUK!!!

All these will serve as a constant reminder of the slim, trim person that you will want and need to be.

Although you need discipline to realise these goals, there is no benefit to being manic about them.

Stress is one of the most prevalent causes of

sickness, both mental and physical. People don't talk about being 'sick with worry' for nothing.

An excess of worry, financial or otherwise, eventually causes nervous breakdowns. So be relaxed about your goals.

There are two essential ways to lose weight; healthy eating and exercise. But there are other ways, too.

For instance, instead of shoveling food into your mouth while watching television or eating with your nose in a smartphone while chatting to your Facebook or Instagram friends, eat *slowly*.

Take your time. Savour each mouthful.

That way, you will find that you eat less and that healthy food is actually much tastier than junk food.

As you turn more and more to salads, fruit, vegetables, nuts and seeds, and drink tea rather than coffee, you will actually begin to dislike the taste of greasy chips, burgers made from slaughter house scraps and overly spiced chicken pieces.

You might question *why* these junk foods are highly spiced. Could it be to disguise the fact that on their own they are as good as tasteless because they are of inferior quality?

Most junk food - including chocolates and candies stacked on endless retailers' shelves - contain huge quantities of sugar or salt to enhance the taste. Both are detrimental to your health in excess.

The good news is that the transition from junk food to healthy food will automatically help you to lose weight, too.

The Huge Benefits of Meditation

The combination of healthy eating and exercise can also be heightened by one of the best ways to relax and de-stress - meditation.

Many people - especially young people - consider meditation to be a bit weird and off the wall. It's not! It's one of the greatest benefits to health available to us.

Simply by sitting upright in a chair for 15-20 minutes once a day, closing your eyes and concentrating on your in- breaths and out-breaths, you will find your entire body relaxes and elevates you to a higher state of consciousness.

You will feel immediately better, creative, raring to go.

Instead of concentrating on your breathing, some people repeat a mantra - ideally any combination of two syllables that do not constitute an actual word. A mantra can be anything: millim, roline, karum - or even just 'Don't Think'.

If you choose this path, you just need to stick to the same mantra, which will then become embedded in your mind.

The repetition of a mantra acts as a brake on your mind. It stops it temporarily from thinking. Thoughts will still emerge like bubbles from mud, but then the mantra takes over again.

The value of these 'rest periods' for the mind are cumulative and over the weeks, months and years, will have a remarkable effect on your entire health and demeanour.

You will develop a relaxed, laid back but extremely positive approach to life - and that is exactly what you want.

There are entire libraries of evidence proving that regular meditation helps to reduce high blood pressure, stress and anxiety.

It also improves the health of your heart and immune system, combats depression and chronic pain and spawns a sense of well-being and happiness.

And One Last Thing...

What we are striving for here is a *balanced* diet and little or no negative stress. If you become fixated about losing weight, the chances are that you will actually end up increasing it.

I know from experience! There have been times when I have eaten virtually nothing all day - a banana for breakfast, a mug of tomato soup for lunch and steamed vegetables for supper - and walked five miles.

Then, the next morning, I've been horrified to see that my weight had *increased* by a pound and a quarter.

So, the message is: Take it easy. Eat sensibly and exercise in moderation.

You may have noticed that when mentioning the importance of exercise, I did not mention going to the gym.

That's partly because if you start muscle building, for example, you are likely to increase your weight.

More importantly, the membership of a gym costs money. And *that* is money you could be saving!

So What Have We Learned This Time?

1. To make a list of your goals - what you want to do with your money when you become wealthy.

2. The *real* reasons for wanting to make money - security, watching your investments grow and the value of giving.

3. How the Law of Attraction works. And why it needs you to be specific about your goals.

4. To think positively and avoid moaners, complainers and other negative people.

5. To never lose faith in yourself and your abilities no matter how much life seems to be going 'against' you.

6. To accept the give and take of life and to be as flexible as water that can be moved easily or wear away the greatest obstacles.

7. To remember that the route to your success can be like a yacht tacking before the wind.

8. How life comes to help you if you don't push it.

9. How by constantly reminding yourself of your goals gradually creates a deep-seated belief in your mind that those goals will become reality.

10. How a healthy diet and moderate exercise create a healthy and creative mind.

11. That meditation is a huge benefit to combating illness, boosting your creativity and attaining a state of well-being.

-£££-

Chapter Five

YOUR FIRST
INVESTMENT FUND

It's time to start! Let's begin by reminding ourselves of how your savings can make you rich assuming you make no withdrawals. The chart below is calculated at a very conservative compound interest of 5%. (Most other authors calculate this at 10%!)

Monthly Savings	10 years	20 years	30 years	40 years	50 years
£ 50	£ 7,924	£ 20,831	£41,856	£76,103	£131,889
£100	£15,848	£ 41,663	£83,712	£152,207	£263,778
£150	£23,772	£ 62,494	£125,569	£228,311	£395,667
£200	£31,696	£ 83.326	£167,425	£304,415	£527,556
£300	£47,554	£124,989	£251,138	£456,623	£791,335
£400	£63,392	£166,6252	£334,851	£608,830	£1,055,133
£500	£79,240	£208,315	£418,564	£761,038	£1,318,892

Of course, you would not expect to be able to put aside £150 or more a month at the age of 16-18, or perhaps even 21. But the table shows how, if you set aside 15% of your higher salary, you will eventually reap a rich harvest!

As we have seen, all you have to do is sit back and forget about it.

Needless to say, having now implanted the firm belief that you *will* be wealthy and perhaps even a millionaire, you will be more alert to the coincidences and opportunities that the Law of Attraction presents to you - and will consequently be able to invest much more.

We seen earlier how you should initially:

1. Set up a bank account

2. Save every penny you can!

3. Set up an ISA investment account, which at the time of writing allows you to invest up to £20,000 a year without being taxed on your capital gains (i.e. profit on the investments)

4. Select an Index Fund with a ratio of 60%-40% stocks to bonds into which you can invest your money

5. Set up a Standing Order or preferably a Direct Debit so that your monthly saving rate is automatically transferred to the Index Fund in your ISA account.

6. When you reach the £20,000 limit in your ISA, buy into another index fund to diversify.

How To Set Up An ISA Account

There are two types of ISA - a cash ISA and an investment ISA. Forget about the first. You want the investment ISA.

You can only buy into an ISA if you are a citizen of the United Kingdom. In America, you would have the option of a similar tax efficient fund called an IRA or Roth IRA.

There are plenty of websites to guide you as to the comparative benefits of these.

As I said before there are any number of investment companies with whom you can choose to invest. Hargreaves Lansdown, Schwab, Blackrock, Morningstar, Schroder, Fidelity, Vanguard, Jupiter, Franklin Templeton, Invesco Perpetual, HSBC, Aberdeen and iShares are just a few of them.

If you google *https://www.money.co.uk/savings-*

accounts/investment-isas, you can see comparisons between the minimum amounts required by different investment companies when opening an ISA account.

At the time of writing, Hargreaves Lansdown, for example, require an investment of a £25 a month, Legal & General ask for £20 a month.

Some companies allow you to open an ISA with no lump sum and no minimum monthly contribution.

However, the lower the amount required, the fewer investment funds are available to choose from - and that seriously curtails your investment strategy and could be decisive in terms of the returns your make on your investment.

In terms of fees, aim for 0.25% or less.

It's Your Choice

It would be unfair and possibly illegal for me to advise you as to which company you should choose. All I can do is to tell you what I have done - and you should not take that in any way, shape or form to be financial advice.

I chose Fidelity, which is one of the oldest asset management companies in the world. Based in Boston, Massachusetts, it is the fourth largest asset manager with $2.4 trillion in assets under management as of January 2018.

If you opt to do as I have done, go to the UK website at fidelity.co.uk. Scroll down and next to the 'Log In' box, you will see an 'Open an account' box.

Click on that and you will be offered a choice of two ISAs. Click on 'Fidelity Investment ISA.' and fill in your personal details.

At the bottom you will be asked to confirm various points. You don't *have* to read these but I would advise you to do so. Click on 'Next' and continue to follow the instructions.

Once you have set up your account and password, and log in you will be taken to your Account summary. To begin with it will be all zeros!

Setting Up Your Direct Debit.

Click on 'My accounts' at the top right of the page. Then click on 'Manage Investments'. You can then choose to add cash to your account or to set up a Regular savings plan, which is absolutely the best way to go ahead.

Choose the maximum amount of money you think you can possibly save on a monthly basis, fill in the other data, then scroll down and you will see your account listed. Click on 'Manage' and then 'Edit Plan'.

You will then be able to choose whether you want the money to be held as cash or invested directly into a fund of your choosing. To begin with, choose 'cash'.

Congratulations! You now have an investment account and you have also set up a Direct Debit so that the amount you have chosen will automatically be deducted from your bank account each month.

In time, you won't even notice it has gone. Once the money has landed, which will be almost instantaneously, you will see the amount listed on your account summary. Beneath the 'Add Cash' box you will see an 'Invest Now' box.

This may not immediately show the amount you have transferred. As soon as it does, usually after two or three days, you will be able to start choosing which investment fund you would like.

Incidentally, if the amount does not show in the 'Invest Now' box immediately, it is because Fidelity have noted that you want to add the amount to your account but have not yet received it from your bank.

Now, the fun begins!

Choosing Your First Investment

The first investment I made was in the Vanguard Life Strategy 60% Index fund. This is an index fund comprising 60% major American companies (equities) and 40% bonds, which tend to act as a hedge when stocks take a dive - as they almost certainly will at some stage.

In fact, you should expect the stock market to fall by up to 10% at least once each year. The trick is not to panic, to ignore the doom and gloom hype in the press and to forget about your investment.

Take a look at it after ten years and you will see that the 60-40% balance has stood you in good stead.

Later in life, you may want to be more cautious, so you could choose a 40-60% stocks to bond ratio. There is even a 20%-80% version, but if there is a bond crisis, the 20% stocks would probably not be enough to protect you.

A fund like one of these is a good, safe bet to start you off. Later, of course, you can change your investment at any time.

The important thing is to buy into a fund immediately so that you can begin to make money - literally while you get on with your life and forget about it.

Needless to say, you are not going to make a fortune immediately. But even if you put away only £25 a month, you are on your way and when you get a job you will be able to afford more.

Every time you get an increase in pay, set aside more from the top and increase your monthly payment. If you are given money as a birthday or Christmas present - save and invest it.

Make saving rather than spending a habit. That way you will see your money grow much more quickly.

The Ultimate Goal

Your ultimate aim, of course, is gradually to build up a portfolio of maybe 10 to 14 funds, covering a sensible ratio of stocks to bonds.

These will cover all kinds of business *sectors* of the market such as banking, food and beverages, aerospace, agriculture, chemicals, computers and construction, the arms industry, energy, and so on.

Your aim will also be to diversify not only across different sectors but also in different parts of the world - Asia, Japan, the Pacific ex-Japan, the UK, Europe, North America and Latin America.

You will also be investing in the developed world and the emerging markets world.

The latter often present the best opportunities because as companies first venture out into the market their prices tend to be low - so you would be betting on their success and consequent growth.

At the moment, my own portfolio is roughly 44% stocks, 46% bonds and 10% commodities,.

The latter consist of a fund called Carmignac Portfolio Commodities which aims to achieve long-term asset growth by passively managing a portfolio of investments in various business segments of the commodity sector.

In other words it tracks different indexes, including oil and gas, energy equipment, metal and mining, paper and forest products, and food.

These ratios are known as 'weighting'. As I write, my portfolio is probably too heavily weighted in favour of stocks and is in need of re-balancing, of which more later.

The Benefits of Youth

Usually, young people tend to opt for more

aggressive stocks, often called 'dynamic' stocks, and your ratio would perhaps be 70% or even 80% weighted in this way.

That way, you make money faster but also increase your risk. If the market suddenly drops by 10%, as it frequently does - at least temporarily - you would not be sufficiently protected.

By the time you reach your thirties, you would probably want to be more cautious. Certainly no more than 60% stocks and at least 40% bonds.

Remember: Bonds are Boring. They don't make you a fortune but usually they do grow your money steadily and at a fixed interest. In other words, they are a 'hedge' against dips in the market.

When you reach your 50s, you will want to protect your nest egg as much as possible because now, you are thinking about retirement - something very few teenagers ever contemplate. At that stage of life, most people would probably opt for a 50-50%, or even 40%-60% ratio of stocks to bonds

If I had started saving and investing two, three, four or even five decades ago, I would be a rich man now. But then I didn't start until I was 81 years old.

That severely limits the time I have available to generate a fortune, so for the moment, I am being more aggressive than perhaps I should be.

Why Markets Rise and Fall

Unfortunately, stock markets are governed by fear and greed. What investors fear most is bad news. A downturn in the economy, high unemployment, high interest rates making borrowing more expensive, a crash in the housing market or the possibility of conflict.

All these and other negative developments in different fields affect whether markets rise or fall.

Uncertainty also creates fear. Take, for example, the Brexit referendum in the United Kingdom.

Businesses had no idea what the government was planning - some would say if it was planning at all. That uncertainty had a devastating effect on the value of the pound sterling and exports, and created an era of almost unparalleled negativity.

The only upside was that with a weak pound, Britain became a good place in which to invest because costs were lower. The media, or course, focused on the doom and gloom aspects of Brexit. Bad news sells newspapers. Good news very rarely.

"Project Fear" - Buzzword of 2017-2019

The uncertainty created by the Brexit vote was such that people immediately began imagining the worst possible outcomes.

The vote was close, splitting the nation by just a few percentage points. Those who had voted to remain in the European Union refused to accept the result achieved by a majority of 17 million people who wanted to leave.

So the 'Remainers' (or 'Remoaners') as they became known began to warn of the terrible consequences of leaving.

British people would have to have visas to travel to Europe and vice versa, they said.

Aircraft would not be allowed to fly over Europe.

Customs and Excise would not be able to process lorries entering or leaving for the continent. The M20 to the Channel Tunnel and the Port of Dover would be gridlocked permanently.

Everything in Britain would cost more. We'd be cast into poverty and deprivation for decades to come.

Oh, My Goodness, we'd all be cutting our throats in despair if you listened to everything they claimed. Britain would be a third rate country with no future, cast into darkness until Kingdom Come.

It was a load of nonsense, of course.

In the 1980's, when stockpiles of coal began to run out., we had a four day week. Electricity - heating and lighting - were effectively rationed.

The streets were piled high with rubbish because there were no garbage collections. People talked of rats infesting our towns. In some parts of the country, you couldn't bury your grandmother.

The media had a wonderful time forecasting the end of the world as we knew it. Yet we survived. As we always survive - and prosper!

Up, Down, Round and Round

Life, as I said, has its ups and downs - and when you have a down, the markets tumble. People lose money because they panic and sell on a falling market -- then, when things improve and the markets rise again, they get hopeful and buy too late.

Changes in ideological and ethical thinking can also be bad news.

For example, if a government suddenly decreed that cement was as dangerous to health as asphalt and banned it in all new buildings, the housing market would collapse.

Similarly with plastic bags. As I write these words now, there has been a change of heart around the world.

For years, companies worldwide and especially in Asia have produced plastic bags. Millions upon millions of them.

Every time anybody bought a couple of apples from the supermarket, they came out with a plastic bag, which they threw away when they got home. Or simply chucked out of their car windows along with KFC packaging.

Garbage collection organisations dump countless tons of plastic into landfill sites or into the sea every week. Gradually, the oceans became awash with plastic bags. I lecture on cruise ships and have seen first hand how the Pacific Ocean, especially, is contaminated by plastic bags. Hundreds of thousands of them.

Fish, sharks, porpoises, dolphins - even whales are dying because of them.

So now there is a worldwide movement to ban plastic bags or at least to produce completely recyclable plastic bags.

This change in our ethical thinking, in our genuine concern for the safety of the planet will undoubtedly have a massive effect, worldwide, on peoples jobs, on the profits of the companies that make plastic bags and ultimately on the plastics sector of the financial markets.

How do you protect yourself against all this?

The answer is to create an investment portfolio that will survive all situations, so that if the economy of one part of the world collapses, you investment in another part of it will balance it out.

This diversification should, as we have already seen, continue across stocks, bonds, commodities and gold.

Furthermore, stocks, bonds and commodities in your portfolio should *each* also be widely diversified.

The overall balance should not just be spread across different parts of the world, but also across many different sectors (aerospace, agriculture, banking etc) and companies with huge amounts of capital (large cap), and medium and 'small cap' companies.

So, to ensure the maximum protection, by the time you are 50-55 years old you should ideally have a portfolio weighted at approximately 30% stocks, 50% bonds and 10% commodities, all diversified as explained, and as a final safeguard, perhaps 10 % gold.

What Kind of Funds Should You Invest In?

There are many thousands of funds from which to choose and that can be a daunting prospect.

So we are faced with a process of choosing by elimination. Just as detectives question suspects 'in order to eliminate them from their enquiry', so we have to dismiss certain types of funds in order to make the final choice simpler.

In the field of investments you can choose between:

1. Stocks and Bonds
2. Individual Stocks or funds
3. Mutual Funds or Index Funds
4. Income or Accumulation Funds

Stocks or Bonds

This one is easy. We have already established that you should have a mix of both because bonds, which are steady and safer, *tend* to balance the volatility of stocks.

This, however, is not always the case. They can both take a dive, *and* at the same time. As a general rule, though, if you are investing passively, which is to say choosing well initially and holding indefinitely, you should have at least 10%-15% more bonds in your portfolio than stocks.

If you prefer to take the risk in the hopes of earning more money faster, then you would reverse that percentage in favour of stocks - and good luck! It's a gamble and it's known as risk tolerance.

Some of the great investors in the world, have figured out that a low-cost portfolio with more bonds than stocks can in certain circumstances actually earn a higher net return than a portfolio with more stocks than bonds.

Individual Stocks or Funds

The difference here is that if you choose to invest in individual stocks, you have to do all the work.

You would need to look at hundreds, if not thousands, of companies, and read their annual reports (with a cynical eye because annual accounts can be manipulated to make the prospects look better).

You would also have to read reports from financial newspapers and online companies offering investment analyses - companies like Morningstar - to search for hidden discrepancies and any negative or dubious aspects to the companies' prospects.

Finally, you would need to check all kinds of indicators for each individual company, such as the earnings per share (EPS), Price to earnings ratio (P/E), the cyclical-defensive ratio, Price to earnings ratio to growth ratio (PEG), Price to book value ratio (P/B), Dividend payout ratio (DPR), and the Dividend Yield.

Multiply that lot by thousands of companies and you can imagine what a massive challenge investing in individual stocks presents.

It's why people go to a broker, whose associates help take away the pain.

But despite their analytical prowess, it has been proved time and time again that brokers are often no better at choosing the right stocks than someone making a choice by stabbing a pin into a long list of stocks.

Furthermore, if your broker has itchy fingers and switches funds too often, you would also have to pay transaction fees and potential capital gains taxes, which would eat away at your profits.

Should I Choose Mutual or Index Funds?

We have already discussed how actively managed mutual funds rarely outperform the market because of high fees, hidden fees and managers frenetically buying and selling stock.

All in order to compete with other managers and consequently accumulating transaction fees and capital gains taxes, as well.

On average, the difference earned by actively managed equity funds after taxes was two per cent less than index funds.

If you invested an initial compounded investment of, say £10,000 between 1990 and 2018, the actively managed fund would have paid about £30,000 less than the Index Fund.

So, it is really a no brainer.

'INC' OR 'ACC'?

Most Funds, mutual or otherwise, usually come in two versions: Income and Accumulative usually referred to as 'Inc' and 'Acc' funds.

An *income* fund will distribute any interest or dividends (i.e. profit) from the fund directly to your bank account, assuming you have given your bank details to the investment company, which is the sensible thing to do.

The idea here is to use your investment to supplement your normal income. This is especially attractive if you are trying to pay off a mortgage or when you reach retirement age.

An *accumulation* fund, on the other hand, is designed automatically to re-invest any interest or dividends, thus increasing the value of your nest egg so that even greater value can be compounded.

The power of compounding also means that if, for example, you invested £10,000 in an accumulation fund and kept it for 20 years, you could, depending on the success of the fund, be between £10,000 and £27,000 better off than if you had invested it in an income fund.

In short, if you are young and want to amass a fortune, you should clearly opt for an accumulation fund. You should only invest in an income fund if you need to rely on extra income for your day-to-day living expenses.

Never Invest In Funds Because They Performed Well in the Past

A word of warning.

If you begin to read financial publications and check out investment companies and their advice online (and you have absolutely no need to do so), you will find yourself tempted by all kinds of hot tips and 'Best Performing Funds' in the previous year, or currently.

It can be a bad mistake to be persuaded by these articles.

That's because funds are run by managers and managers on average only last for around eight to ten years.

So if a fund has performed brilliantly for eight years, beware! The new manager may not be quite so sharp.

Every financial newspaper, book or online website will print - usually in small print - that past performance is no guarantee of future performance, that investments can go up as well as down (and certainly down as well as up!)

In his excellent publication *The Little Book of Common Sense Investing,* John Bogle checked out the 46 year record of 355 equity funds since 1970.

What he found was that 281 of those funds had gone out of business. That's 80% of them.

And of those 355 funds, only *two* beat the market by

more than 2%, and eight by 1%.

As Bogle wrote so wisely: "The stars produced in the mutual fund field rarely remain stars; all too often they become meteors.

How Long Can A Five-Star Rated Fund Stay That Way?

The smart investor will avoid choosing five-star rated mutual funds simply on the basis of the past long or short-term performance.

They will certainly avoid professional and persuasive advice from fund managers who claim their funds will outpace the market.

Instead, I can't impress upon you enough that investing in low-cost index funds that track the FTSE 100, FTSE 250, S&P 500 or other similar indexes and sticking with them through thick and thin, is the safest and almost certainly most profitable way to go.

Coming Soon? Fee Free Index Funds?

In the United States, Fidelity has recently introduced onto the New York Stock Exchange two index funds - the Fidelity Zero Total Market Index Fund and the Fidelity Zero International Index Fund - with no management fees at all.

Unfortunately, these are not available in Britain, where Fidelity operates only with the London Stock Exchange.

But Fidelity is the first investment company to do this and it will also lower fees on other funds by an average 35%.

Even better for the young investor, they will charge no investment minimums to access these lower and no-fee funds.

So, you can be sure that in time, these innovations will spread to the United Kingdom.

Let's Recap on What We Have Learned Again

1. That the earlier you start saving and investing, and the more you add to your investment pot as your salary increases, the faster you will achieve wealth for life.

2. To set up a bank account and an ISA account as soon as possible. Do it now!

3. How to choose your first investment index fund, preferably one that has a 60%-40% or 40%-60% ratio of stocks and bonds such as a Vanguard LifeStrategy fund.

4. How to create the ultimate investment portfolio.

5. How to protect your portfolio against all eventualities.

6. Why markets fall.

7. The kind of funds in which to invest.

8. The difference between stocks and bonds.

9. The advantage of index funds over actively managed funds.

10. The contrasting benefits of income and accumulation funds.

11. Never rely on past performance when choosing an investment.

12. Why actively managed funds are costly and don't last.

-£££-

Chapter Six

STRATEGIES FOR THE FUTURE

There is no sure fire way of how you should or should not spread your assets. Much depends on your age, your temperament and how long you have available to invest.

Teenagers, students and young people in their twenties, will want to be more aggressive in their investment strategy, growing net worth with a long-term outlook and being prepared to take a fair amount of risk. This might suggest a portfolio split between 10% dynamic growth 45% growth, 20% growth and income, 15% bonds and 10% cash.

It is always a good idea to keep some cash around because when markets fall they presents excellent opportunities to buy good bargains at a low price.

When you are earning more in your 30s and 40s (when your risk tolerance his high) you might well want to concentrate more on building up your fortune as quickly as possible.

In thist case, a good spread might be 10% dynamic growth, 30% growth, 30% growth and income, 20% bonds and 10% cash

Similarly, when you are approaching retirement in your 50s and 60s, your strategy will change again. By then you will almost certainly be achieving your peak salary at a time when, hopefully, your outgoings will be fewer.

You would be thinking much more about your retirement and would increasingly want to safeguard your investments.

That would call for very little aggressive growth - 5% tops. You would probably opt for as little as 35% growth and 50% bonds, 5% commodities, 5% gold and

5% cash.

Finally, when you reach your 60s you would want as little risk as possible and to protect what you have accumulated over the years.

At this point, you would switch to almost no aggressive growth, 35% growth, 55% bonds and 10% cash or gold.

These, of course, are all perfectly acceptable financial strategies. But they are not strategies that will protect you through thick and thin.

How to Achieve a Near Perfect Spread

Achieving the most appropriate - and safest - balance is not rocket science. Let's assume you create a portfolio comprising:

· US, UK, European and Asian stock indexes,

· Emerging market indexes from the same geographical areas,

· At least 15% more bond indexes than stock indexes, also from the same geographical regions, and

· Finally add in a commodity index and maybe a gold index or even physical gold.

Needless to say, there is no perfect asset spread. The nearest you can get to one would, as an example, be index funds comprising 30%-35% stocks, 55%-50% bonds, 5% commodities and 10% cash.

Having cash is important. If everything goes pear shaped and the market crashes, you need to have cash to buy the really low priced bargains that become available - because eventually the cyclical pattern ensures that these *will* eventually rise again.

If you leave a portfolio such as this alone and do absolutely nothing to it for 40, 50, or even 60 years, you will almost certainly survive all eventualities in the long term, including market crashes, recessions, four-day weeks, and so on.

That means you never need to read the financial newspapers and magazines. You never have to concern yourself about impending rate rises, inflation, unemployment, how the national economy is doing or the effect of world events on the financial world.

You just don't, ever, need to panic, far less worry - and a financially stress free life is worth a pot of gold in itself.

The Importance of Re-Balancing

It sounds idyllic and in many ways it is. There is just one more challenge in this financial minefield.

Let's assume you have invested £5,000 in each of the following accumulative funds:

US Equity Index, Emerging Markets Index(ASIA), Japan stock Index, FTSE All Share Index, Developed Europe ex UK Index, UK government Bond index, Global Bond Index, Euro Government Bond index, Japan Government Bond index, and a commodities index.

After six months or a year, it would be a miracle if these had grown equally. Some might be worth £5,500 others £4,750. Perhaps more, perhaps less, depending on external influences.

If your original - and excellent - balance was 30% stocks, 55% bonds and 7.5% commodities and 7.5% gold, you could well discover after six months or a year that some stocks and commodities had soared while your bonds had dipped.

So, now your balance might be more like 45% stocks and 30% bonds and 25% commodities and gold.

If you allowed that to happen indefinitely, you would no longer have a balanced portfolio. So, you need to re-balance.

Failure to re-balance can be a little dangerous. It is

certainly not impossible that you might be tempted to stick with what you have.

After all, if the stocks and commodities are doing just great, why not stick with them?

Oh dear! You have just fallen into the ever-present trap of believing that a rising market will continue forever. You've allowed your emotions to take control.

And that, of course, is when the crash comes. Remember, the whole purpose of a balanced portfolio is to protect you against just such occasions. This is where you need discipline, the resolve to stick with your original asset allocation and a firm belief that average growth is just great!

Is Selling A Rising Star Such A Bad Idea?

Sometimes, this means that you would need to sell off some of the rising stock indexes in order to *reduce* your risk and invest the money back into those bond index funds that are not doing so well so that you can continue to maintain a portfolio that will carry you through all situations.

Selling off a winning ticket may seem a crazy idea, but it's not so dumb if you want to hedge your bets and cover yourself so that you can weather future storms and maybe a sudden dive in the next few days or even hours.

When that happens, you've missed the boat.

Remember the diagram of rising and falling emotions on page 21? The 'BUY! BUY!" Wow, I'm Making mega-bucks' syndrome? Never forget that markets move in repetitive waves.

To be disciplined enough to resist the temptation to hang on for too long takes courage - but that's what makes a really great investor!

I know you won't want to do it, but it is absolutely *crucial* that you *do* because it is the only protection you can get.

Re-balancing doesn't always work, but if you are investing for the long term, the likelihood is that you will gain far more often than you will lose.

And that means the chances of your overall success are infinitely greater.

How Often Should I Re-balance?

There are no rules about how often you should re-balance. It is entirely up to you. Some people re-evaluate their portfolios almost every week or month, but there's no point in becoming obsessive about it.

Other people leave it for one or two years, preferring to let the investments continue as they are for a while, rather than selling just because the price is rising.

On average, I intend to re-balance at least once a year and perhaps every six months.

Re-balancing is a powerful tool because it not only protects you from excessive risk, it can actually *increase* your profits.

You may well be moving into an asset that is not performing as well as it should. That's why it's cheap!

But if, as happens so often, it begins to improve and even outperform the markets, then you would have bought yourself a bargain.

Of course, the downside of re-balancing is that you may have to pay transaction fees and capital gains tax on any sales. But overall, that is a minor consideration.

That is especially true if you are young because as I mentioned earlier, you don't pay capital gains on the first £11,700 of your profits.

Maximise Your Profits, Minimize Your Losses

The concept of selling when prices are high and

buying at the bottom of the market is ideal but difficult to judge.

How do you know whether a stock or fund will *continue* to rise? That's what we all hope, but hope is an emotion and emotions have no place in successful investing.

Similarly, how do you know how long a stock or fund will continue to fall? Where is the bottom of the wave?

One way of flattening out the difference is cost averaging.

In other words, if you make regular monthly contributions to your portfolio, you will average out the cost over time.

Sometimes, you will invest your monthly payment when the purchase price is low and at others when it is high.

In fact, some investors believe that cost averaging can actually increase the value of your portfolio by as much as 1% because buying at a bargain price can outweigh the higher cost of buying at the top of the cyclical curve.

The other advantage of cost averaging is that you can use the monthly payments to help re-balance your portfolio.

Tax-Loss Harvesting

There is also a completely legal method of re-balancing a portfolio whilst at the same time reducing your capital gains taxes.

Americans call it 'tax loss harvesting'. In the United Kingdom, it's known as 'Allowable Losses'.

Tax authorities in the U.K. levy a capital gains tax, currently set at 20%, on the profits that you make on your investments whenever you sell them.

This, of course, does not apply if you have invested them in an ISA.

What 'allowable losses' means is that if, for example, you have invested in funds that have lost money, you can sell them and use those losses to offset other capital gains.

You can then replace the sold funds with similar ones and thus maintain an ideal asset allocation and expected returns.

All you have to do is to remember to claim the losses from the taxman, which is another reason for re-balancing your portfolio each year and thus checking to see which funds are losing money.

Incidentally, you do not pay capital gains tax on assets that you give or sell to your husband, wife or civil partner - provided that you did not separate and live elsewhere at any time in that tax year or give them assets for their businesses to sell on.

You also do not have to pay capital gains tax on any assets you give to charity.

The Blight of Taxes

Governments need vast amounts of money to pay for a country's infrastructure - roads, railways, street lighting and so on. So, they levy taxes on everything you earn and most of what you buy, including your pensions.

Many people say this is nefarious because they have already paid on their earnings, so why, they argue, should they have to pay on the pensions, which they have managed to create from savings.

They have a point but there is nothing we can do about it. Look instead on the bright side and you will find that the government believes it is in *their* interest for you to invest your money.

Not only are they able to collect capital gains taxes

on your profits but they also benefit because people who invest their money are not so dependent on the state when they eventually become wrinklies.

Nonetheless, taxation does eat away at your savings and investments like mice with a wedge of Cheddar.

So it pays to plan. As we have seen, ISAs (IRAs or Roth IRAs) offer the best way to protect your money from Capital Gains taxes.

Putting stock and bond index tracking funds in your ISA will almost guarantee a significant boost to your returns in the long term.

Taxation and Pensions

Teenagers and students understandably have little interest in pensions and even adults in their 30s and 40s pay little heed to them. That, as they say, is not a good career move.

Employers usually operate pension schemes and these are something to be considered because your contributions are deducted automatically, so as with the 15% you cream off your salary to put towards your investments, you don't really miss them.

Not everybody is in favour of occupational pension schemes, not least because in recent years, many companies have been found to have spent the money and consequently find themselves with millions - even billions - of pounds 'missing'.

An alternative to an employer's pension scheme is to start a personal pension or a self-invested personal pension (SIPP).

Whatever type of pension you eventually opt for, it will offer relief from income tax. In that respect, they are in some ways similar to ISAs.

As you save over the years, you pay no tax on the gains. You only pay tax when you reach retirement age and start to draw an income from your pension fund.

You would also be able to withdraw a lump sum of up to 25% of your pension fund free of tax.

So, like everything else, the earlier you begin, the more you win.

Inheritance Tax

As with pensions, the idea of anyone aged under 30 even thinking about inheritance tax and how to avoid taxes on their death bed is to stretch the imagination to its limits.

So, it might be an idea to read this book a couple of times, absorb the messages and then lock it away to be read again on your 30th and 40 birthdays.

Benjamin Franklin, once said that there are only two certainties in life. Death and taxes. Ronald Reagan added that it was a pity they don't come in that order!

Unfortunately, even as your family mourn you on your death bed, the tax man is hovering in the background.

The moment you die, your estate - the value of all your assets - is assessed in a process known as probate, which determines how much the taxman will take.

You do not currently pay inheritance tax on the first £325,000 per person. This doubles to £650,000 for a married couple but only as long as the first person to die leaves their entire estate to their partner.

Anything over this limit is subject to a 40% tax bill, although you can avoid paying some of this tax, for instance, if you make gifts to charities.

Trust Funds

You could also set up a trust fund which avoids the probate process altogether.

Basically, a trust means that you can place your

money, investments, home, land, expensive paintings and other assets into a separate fund, which is controlled by trustees who, on your death, pass them on to the beneficiaries of your choice.

There are several different types of trusts and setting one up is a highly complex process demanding the expertise of a solicitor or financial advisor or both at a very considerable cost.

You would expect to pay a minimum fee of £3,000 and some firms offering these services ask for extortionate amounts of up to £15,000. So, you need to do some research and shop around.

As trusts avoid the probate procedure altogether, it means that you can protect your assets and control who gets what and under what conditions.

For instance, you could leave money to a young person whom you consider too young to be sensible with money or, if they are incapacitated in some way, so that they cannot have access to it until a certain age, or perhaps only in specific amounts per month.

The downside is that once you have placed your assets in a trust fund they are no longer yours. The trustees become the legal owners of the assets.

Their job is to make sure the terms of the settlor's (grantor's in the U.S.) wishes are carried out to the letter. They must also manage the trust on a day-to-day basis and pay any tax that is due.

They also decide how to invest the assets, although you can leave specific instructions on this as well.

It is permissible to have just one trustee but as a safeguard it is wise to name more than one.

Beneficiaries can be a single person or a group of people. For instance, if in the unhappy event that your married son suddenly left his wife and four children, you could make explicit directions to exclude him from any benefits.

Instead, you could leave a specific amount to be divided equally (or even unequally) between his ex-wife and four children.

You might also direct that these amounts be paid either as a lump sum or as a regular income, and either immediately or   at a certain age, or specify that the money be used solely for the children's education or other designated purpose.

Similarly, if you had placed a holiday home that you rent out in the trust, you could direct that one beneficiary should own the house and that another should receive the rentals from it - although that, of course, could be a recipe for trouble!

To repeat: Setting up a trust fund is extremely complicated and should only be executed through a solicitor or financial advisor..

Exchange-Traded Funds.

Aside from actively managed funds and passive, low-cost index funds that you buy and hold for the long term, there are also exchange-traded funds, target date funds and high yield bonds to consider. I mention these only because it is advisable to know what they are and how they work - and why you don't necessarily need to bother with them.

Exchange trading funds, commonly known as ETFs have become hugely popular in recent years.

They are pretty much the same as index funds in that they comprise a diversified selection of assets at a very low cost.

There are, however, two crucial differences.

The first is that if you want to buy or sell an index fund, you have to wait until the markets close. ETFs on the other hand can be traded at any time of the day.

So you can sit in front of a computer and watch the

price charts fluctuating from one minute to the next.

You can use artificial intelligence software to buy and sell on rising or falling markets and maybe make some big gains. Or not! The risk of trading like this is huge because it is speculative - the very aspect of investing that you want to avoid.

The second and perhaps most important difference is that with a passive index fund you own the *actual* stocks, bonds and commodities within the fund. This is not true of the ETF.

With the latter, you are buying shares *only* in the investment fund itself, not the specific assets in the fund.

That means it can be almost impossible to compare your returns with those gained in the stock market.

What's more, this all too often results in a shortfall between what you get and the ETF's returns. Sometimes this shortfall can be more than 10% a year.

Frenzied Trading Again!

When you buy into an ETF that is becoming more and more actively managed, you may find that the management fees are low, but remember the transaction fees will add up.

You may also find it significant that approximately 50% of all ETFs are held by banks, fund managers and professional traders who, as we have seen, mostly trade frenetically to keep ahead of the next financial wizard.

If you do consider buying into ETFs, remember to keep your emotions in check and don't chase the crest of the wave.

Ask yourself also whether the advertised low cost fees might be a diversion to hide the fact that broker's commissions and potential capital gains taxes will be levied each time you buy in the morning and sell at lunchtime.

Not for nothing are ETF's regarded as bonanza time for managers and brokers. Remember, too, that the more aggressive your trading, the more it will cost.

Target-Date Funds

The idea of the target date   fund, or life cycle fund as it is sometimes known, is to choose a date when you expect to retire and let a fund manager adjust your portfolio so that from an aggressive start it gradually becomes less adventurous.

If you have chosen a retirement date, say, 40 years into the future, the fund manager will gradually sell off your initial holdings of stocks, which are considered more risky, and replace them with bonds, which are considered to be safer.

This transition is known as a glide path. The problem here is that each manager has his own method of re-adjusting the portfolio according to his own whims and there are no rules or regulations to govern how he does it.

The Growing Reliance on Artificial Intelligence

The use of artificial intelligence (AI) is used increasingly to re-balance target dated and other funds automatically. This can be beneficial because it eliminates completely the emotional aspects of investing.

For some people, especially if they have no knowledge of how the investment world works, there is no doubt that target date funds are an advantage.

They are simple and demand little or no interaction. You can establish them and then pretty much forget about them until your retirement date.

You don't even need to keep an eye on the portfolio and re-balance it because that is done for you. Once you have a target fund, you can just leave it to make money for you while you sleep.

Other people are wary of target dated funds because they have no input as to how the fund is managed. So perhaps they should ask themselves: "Should I trust a second hand fund manager?"

Of Course, There *Are* Drawbacks!

Stocks and bonds do not necessarily move in opposite directions in a rising or falling market.

Indeed, they can *both* take a dive in a falling market, so you need to be circumspect about the whole concept of investing in aggressive stocks at an early age and gradually switching to bonds later on.

Nor do target funds take into consideration that life sometimes throws surprises at you. What would happen, for instance, if you are unable to save at some point? Perhaps due to illness or being made redundant.

You need to undertake a considerable amount of research before investing in a target date fund because apart from anything else, there are thousands from which to choose.

In any event, you should never expect *all* your retirement income to come from a target fund.

There Are No Guarantees.

Target-date funds don't guarantee a specific rate of return Nor is the target date necessarily the same date - or even year - as your actual retirement.

These funds are no more than a selection of assets chosen by a manager who, by whatever means, allocates them as he sees fit.

They *should* make gains but there are no assurances. It is unlikely but not inconceivable that you could end up with less money than when you started.

High Yield Bonds

You could say that High Yield Bonds are almost a misnomer. Just as there is no such thing as a free lunch, there is no such thing as 'high yield' without risk and potential disaster.

Not for nothing were High Yield Bonds once known as 'junk' bonds.

Yes, they pay a super-attractive high rate of interest, but that in turn means that they have a much lower credit rating than the more stable Treasury, government or corporate bonds, which pay less. Sometimes, less works out as more!

All bonds are rated by Moody's and Standard & Poor's, the world's leading index provider and the foremost source of independent credit ratings . They have been providing market intelligence to financial experts for more than 150 years.

High risk bonds are rated in much the same way as you or me when we apply for a bank loan or credit card. By definition, high risk bonds mean that the company is probably on a financial cliff edge.

The company or organisation offering a high yield bond is unlikely to receive a decent credit rating because although it may be able to meet payments it is likely - in the view of the Moody's or Standard & Poor's - to remain susceptible to adverse business conditions or a poor national economic outlook.

In other words, if business and economic conditions become unfavourable, the company may well default - and you lose your money.

Of course, all companies and all investments are at risk to a greater or lesser extent during an economic downturn.

But at least you have a far greater chance of success and ultimate wealth with a broadly diversified portfolio of low cost, passive target funds or index funds, regularly re-balanced and held for the long term.

What You Have Learned In This Chapter

1. Asset allocations for different age groups.

2. The near perfect asset allocation for long term investment.

3. How stock market movements change the balance of your portfolio and the importance of re-balancing.

4. How often you should re-balance.

5. The benefits of keeping cash in hand and cost averaging.

6. Re-balancing and how to reduce you capital gains tax by loss harvesting (allowable losses).

7. How to beat taxation by putting index funds in your ISA or IRA.

8. The benefits of self-invested personal pensions.

9. The ins and outs of inheritance tax.

10. Why Trust Funds can be a solution to protecting your wealth.

11. The downsides of exchange traded funds.

12. Why target date funds are not always a good idea.

13. To beware of high yield (junk) bonds.

-£££-

Chapter Seven

HOUSES, MORTGAGES AND
THE JOY OF GIVING

One of the most important and profitable moves you can ever make is to invest in a house. Sadly, these days, that is a very difficult proposition for most young people.

The average cost of a house in Britain in the first quarter of 2018 was £227,871, the highest on record. Of course, that figure varies according to where you buy.

Someone once said that you can't buy a garage in London for less than a million pounds. It was a joke, of course, but there was an element of truth in it.

The typical cost of buying house in the UK is now at the 'least affordable level in a decade', according to a Lloyds Bank review.

If you wanted to buy a house in Kensington or Chelsea, for example, you would be looking to pay an *average* £1.8 million, which is not exactly within the reach of your average student.

Conversely, Rightmove's online house price checker shows that in North East England, most property sales in 2018 were semi-detached houses selling on average for £150,223. Terraced houses were selling for around £120,000.

The overall average for the North East, though, was £162,379, whereas in the North West it was £190,804.

First-time buyers should expect to pay a minimum 5% and as much as 25% of the price of a house as a down payment on a mortgage.

That amounts to a monumental £56,967 on a property costing the average £227,871.

If you were buying a house for £120,000 you would need to pay a deposit of between £6,000 and £30,000. A house costing £150,000 would require £7,500 to £37,500.

Throughout Britain, it will take eight to ten years to save up for a mortgage on average, even if you save 15% of your take home pay.

Needless to say, the more you pay up front, the less interest you will pay on the mortgage loan and the faster you will pay it off.

For a 20-year-old working in their first job, even £6,000 is a vast amount of money to find, so no wonder young people find it so difficult to get a mortgage and instead opt to rent an apartment.

Renting versus Buying a Home

Unfortunately renting is a mug's game. When you rent, the only person to get rich is the landlord. Your chances of achieving wealth are zilch.

Consider this: A single person renting a one bedroom flat in East or West London in 2018 could expect to pay between £350 and £450 a month or £450-£600 south of the Thames.

Let's take the medium rent of £400 a month for 30 years, which is a normal length for a mortgage.

That's £144,000 you would have paid to a landlord - and at the end of those 30 years you would have absolutely nothing to show for it.

Compounded, your £400 a month for 30 years would amount to £334,851, but then, of course, you would have to live in a tent for 30 years!

Nonetheless, for £400 a month for 30 years, you could have bought a terraced house in the North East of England and spent £20,000 transforming it into a beautiful, modern home that you would *own* and which would also appreciate in price over the years.

What's more, there would be no landlord to put up your monthly rent and perhaps even evict you if you couldn't afford it.

An even better deal would be if, when you are earning your peak salary, you were able to buy a second home so that *you* could become a landlord.

Then you would have the security of a house, the mortgage of which would have been paid off and a steady monthly income from the rental of the second home, as well.

There are any number of studies to show that those who buy a home end up far wealthier than those who rent, so always think of a mortgage as an *investment* towards your future wealth, rather than as a *debt* that seems almost impossible to pay off.

Still Not Convinced? Look At It This Way!

Let's say you are buying a house - perhaps a semi-detached home in the North East of England - for the current average price of £150,000.

You pay a deposit of 5%, which is £7,500. That means you are using £142,500 of the bank's money to help you buy the house.

In other words, you are borrowing in order to make a profit because at the end of the day, you will own the house. It's called leveraging and the best investors in the world use it whenever it's advantageous.

Ah! I hear you argue - but that's one mother of a debt to have to pay off!

Is it? Think again!

Supposing you bought a semi-detached house in Gateshead, near Newcastle. This is one of the cheapest areas in Britain.

Even if that is still the case in 20 years' time, your £150,000 house would be worth an estimated £555,963.

That means that you would have made a profit of £405,463 on your original £7,500 investment, effectively doubling your money 19 times.

In other words, you bought a house worth well over half a million for just £7,500. The rest of the purchase amount was paid with the bank's money.

Of course, each month you had to pay off a portion of the principal amount of debt and the extortionate interest it accrued.

If you include mortgage repayments at 5% you would pay £237,584 on your £150,000, so by leveraging you would have made a net profit in 20 years of £318,379.

But as we have seen, those payments were not so much paying off a debt as monthly contributions to your own investment account. To put it simply, you were not paying the bank at all. You were paying yourself!

Different Types of Mortgage

There are essentially three different types of mortgage. These are fixed rate mortgages, tracker rate mortgages and variable rate mortgages.

Fixed rate mortgages are when the monthly rate of interest remains the same for a given number of years. The longer you have the loan, the higher the interest is likely to be. But at least you don't have to worry about the Bank of England (or Federal Reserve in the U.S.) raising interest rates.

So there is an element of security in fixed rate mortgages, unlike Tracker mortgages, which can change - usually tracking the national base rate.

Tracker mortgages tend to be less expensive than fixed rate mortgages and may seem a good deal given that the base rate in 2018 was only 0.75% having just increased from 0.50%.

The perceived wisdom is that the Bank of England and Federal Reserve will raise those rates, perhaps significantly to as much as 5% during the next decade. We shall see.

The lowest cost mortgages are those with a variable rate of interest, but these are much riskier because the lender can raise the rate at any time, whether or not the Bank of England or Federal Reserve do so.

A Difference of Tens of Thousands

Choosing the right mortgage is crucial. If you bought a house for the average £227,871 and paid off your fixed rate mortgage at 5% interest, you would be paying £1,224 a month and a total £440,555. That's not far off double the price of your house.

Obviously, keeping your mortgage rate as low as possible is vitally important.

You can do this by paying a larger deposit and thus reducing what is called the loan-to-value. In other words, the remaining amount to pay.

Clearly, if you can only afford to pay a 5% deposit you will end up paying a great deal more than if you paid a 20% deposit. The more you can afford to put down, the less the mortgage will cost and the quicker you will get rid of it.

You could also opt for shorter term mortgages. This means that you can search around for cheaper deals, just as you can with your mobile phone.

By and large, the short term deal is cheaper than longer ones. However, if you switch too frequently you could end up with higher costs.

Mortgages usually come with exit fees and these could mount up if you switched every couple of years. So a two-year deal may not necessarily be better than a five-year deal.

Of course, your mortgage will be calculated on the basis of the full term - 25 or 30 years. But overall, it does pay to re-mortgage at the end of a deal.

But How On Earth Do I Find
The Money For A Deposit?

This is one of the most difficult parts of getting onto the housing ladder and it is the single most common reason for young people to give up on the idea.

That, as you have seen, is a bad mistake - but what can you do about it?

The good news is that are various government and other schemes to help you buy a home.

For instance, there is the Equity Loan scheme, for anyone who wants to buy a 'new build' house costing no more than £600,000.

As long as you can afford to pay a 5% deposit, the scheme allows you to borrow 40% of the purchase price *interest free* for the first five years if you live in London, and 20% elsewhere.

There is also a Starter Home Scheme in which the government is making 200,000 new build homes available to first-time buyers under the age of 40 with at least 20% off the market price.

There is a cap on homes outside London of £250,000 and of £450,000 in London.

You could also consider buying pre-fabricated houses. These range from 'residential cabins of around 6 x 10 metres costing £10,000-£14,000.

Higher up the scale are prefabricated houses costing approximately £70,000 to £250,000.

Other Costs to Consider

Needless to say, there are plenty of other people queuing up to take your money.

First, there is the mortgage lender's booking fee

(£100-£250), an 'arrangement' fee (£2,000) and valuation fee.

The mortgage company will need to assess the value of the property to gauge how much they will lend you. That could cost up to £1,500.

You should pay these extra costs up front, rather than adding them to your mortgage. Otherwise you will end up paying interest on them, as well!

When you buy a house, you also need to pay a surveyor to ensure that everything is as it should be. Surveyor's fees range between about £250 for a basic survey to £600 for a full structural survey.

Then there are the solicitor's fees for conveyancing (i.e. preparing the legal documents).

If you have any furniture, you will need to pay removal costs. Typically, these would be between £850-£1,500.

A local search to see if there are any hidden plans such as allowing new builds to block your view, or new roads about to be built. This will add another £300 or so to your legal bill.

Insurance companies will be waiting in line to insure your house against fire, floods, subsidence and contents.

Unless you are a carpenter and decorator, you will also have furnishing and decorating costs.

You will have removal costs to think about, too. Moving home could cost between £400-£750 depending on distance and other factors.

In total, you could be looking at as much as £10,000 in extra costs.

Stamp Duty - You May Not Have To Pay!

Then there is the dreaded Stamp Duty (known as Land Transaction costs in Scotland and Wales).

However, if you are a first-time buyer and keep the price of your first house below £300,000, you will not have to pay Stamp Duty.

If, in the unlikely event as a 20-year-old, you can afford a house up to £500,000 then you would not pay the first £300,000 Stamp Duty. There are some good websites around that calculate the approximate extra costs for you.

Having taken all these costs into account, you need to be 100% certain that you will be able to afford the monthly repayments.

These days, the mortgage companies carry out strict tests to make sure you would be able to continue paying even if interest rates were to rise .

They would also take into consideration the possibility of your having children, with the additional costs that they would entail.

Homework Isn't Just For School!

When you embark on the house-buying journey, it is essential that you do your homework. There are any number of mortgage companies and they all have slightly different approaches.

As always, some fall into the category of sharks, so it is essential to find out everything you can about mortgages and mortgage brokers.

Learn about the different kinds of mortgage and seek advice from people with experience.

You will need to provide evidence of how much you earn, whether you have any debts (hopefully, if you read this far, you will have only savings!), how much your current household costs are eating into your earnings.

They would also want to know how much you spend on clothes, entertainment, eating out and travel. So, it's important that you keep all your receipts for a year and place them in files under the various headings listed above.

Leasehold or Freehold?

When you buy a house, you will almost certainly be buying the freehold, but with a flat (apartment if you are an American), you will probably have to buy the leasehold.

That means you don't own the flat. You merely pay a landlord to let you live there for a specific length of time.

Clearly, buying a flat is not a good option if you want to be rich. If you still decided to take that route, make sure you have a *long* lease, preferably 99 years.

When you are in your twenties, a 20 or 30 year lease may seem light years into the future but, believe me, the years will pass much quicker than you think. Should you wish to extend a lease, you will find it very costly, not least because the landlord essentially has you over a barrel if you want to stay where you are.

You Could Get Someone Else to Finance You

It is possible, though not necessarily advisable, to secure what is known as a guarantor mortgage. This is when your parents, guardians or close relatives agree to pay the mortgage if you are not able to do so.

However, guarantor mortgages are potentially dangerous arrangements because they are legally binding.

Anyone agreeing to be a guarantor is responsible for paying off the mortgage if the borrower (you) are unable to do so. It is not just a case of giving a character reference. It means that if you default, the mortgage company is entitled to go calling on the guarantor first.

In some cases, there is also a danger of a guarantor unwittingly having to take on any other debts, such as credit card debts, that you might have amassed.

Guarantors do have the right to limit the amount of money guaranteed and it also possible to cancel the guarantee, although that would not release them from the original debt - only any additional debts incurred after the cancellation.

To summarise, guaranteed mortgages are not a good idea unless your parents, guardians or close relatives are wealthy enough not to feel the pain.

The Pain of the 30-Year Mortgage

There are arguments both for and against paying off a mortgage early. Firstly, there are usually penalties for doing so. Sometimes, mortgage companies won't let you.

It is also worth considering whether you might be better off by putting any extra money into an ISA or a pension.

If the financial markets are upbeat and rising, boosting your £20,000 ISA allowance as close to the limit as you can has to be a good move.

Although a 30-year mortgage is cheaper than, say a 20 or 15 year mortgage, the downside is that it takes an age to pay off a long-term mortgage.

That's because you are paying huge amounts to the bank in return for only a little towards your house.

How Much You *Actually* Pay to the Bank

Take for example a £250,000 semi-detached house. With a 30-year mortgage, at 5% interest you would pay £1,342 a month.

Although in 30 years you would have bought a house, you would have paid an average £647 each month in interest, which over the full term would amount to approximately £233,000.

That's 93.3% of the value of your house. In total, you would have paid an awesome £483,000 for your £250,000 house. Two hundred and thirty three thousand smackers to the bank!

It gets worse. If you decided to sell your house after ten years, your monthly payments would have reduced your principal from £250,000 to only £203,355.

You would have paid off only £46,645 or 18.66% of your principal with another 81.34% still to pay. The reason? Because during the first ten or so years of the mortgage, most of the money you pay monthly goes towards the interest, not the principal.

Paying Off Your Mortgage Early

Obviously, it is hugely advantageous if you can pay off your mortgage as fast as possible. There are a few ways you can do that.

Firstly, you can potentially save thousands of pounds by switching from a long-term fixed rate mortgage to a shorter term mortgage at a lower rate of interest.

Secondly, you could pay more each month, assuming your mortgage lender allows this, which is unlikely with a fixed rate mortgage.

If you divide the principal by 12 and add that to your monthly payments, it means that you would be paying 13 monthly payments a year rather than twelve.

If you do opt to do this, make sure you check your monthly statements to see that the extra payment has been correctly applied. Some banks, for example, just hang on to the money and add it on at the end of the current year.

Alternatively, you could just save 1/12th of a month's payment each month, then pay a full extra month at the end of every 12 months.

This, too, will shorten the length of the mortgage and also save you thousands of pounds.

Finally, if you get a bonus at work or win an amount on the lottery (far better to save the money, though, than gamble it away) you could use that money to make an extra payment on the mortgage, provided your mortgage lender allows it.

The Bi-Weekly Payment Plan

One excellent way to bring down the cost and length of a mortgage is to pay half your monthly payment every two weeks.

If you pay monthly, you pay 12 times a year. If you pay bi-weekly, you make 26 payments a year, effectively 13 monthly payments.

It may not sound much but, again, it has the potential to save you tens of thousands of pounds in interest.

For instance, if we take your £250,000 house with a 30-year mortgage at 5% interest again, by paying bi-weekly, you would pay it off nearly five years early and save about £45,000.

You would need to check with your mortgage lender or bank whether they have such a scheme because although it is common practice in the United States, Canada, New Zealand, Australia and other countries, in Britain it is much more difficult.

Be careful, though, and make absolutely sure that the bi-weekly payments are *applied* on a bi-weekly basis to your principal.

Some mortgage companies don't do this. Instead they just hold on to the money for two weeks until the receive the second half of your payment and then apply it to your loan only after they receive the full monthly payment.

Over-paying is Good News - But Watch Out!

You *can*, however, make extra payments in Britain and these can have the same effect. By reducing the monthly amount you shorten the length of the mortgage and thus make savings.

That said, I can't stress enough, that you need to be careful. You need to find out what actually happens to your over-payment and when.

Are there are any fees for setting up an overpayment scheme?

If fees are applied, do they outweigh the benefit of over-paying? You can figure out the sums with a user friendly mortgage over-payment calculator, of which there are several online.

If you opt for over-payments, make sure you know *exactly* when it is applied, whether it is put towards reducing your principal or the interest, or both?

Remember, the financial world is full of profit gobblers more interested in making their own fortunes than yours.

Finally, if you decide to pay an extra monthly payment at the end of the year, don't simply double the amount as this would leave the lender bewildered.

Instead, write out two cheques for your monthly payment amount and make sure your lender is aware that you want it to pay off the *principal* - and request confirmation in writing that this has occurred.

Enough!

Understandably, you may feel that with all the fees and costs, greedy fund managers and the feeling that trying to get a mortgage is akin to drowning in a swamp, you just want to give up.

Don't!

Think of the power of compounding. Re-read Chapter One.

Think of the huge investment you are making.

Think of saving every penny, every cent, every zloty, krona, rouble, washer or whatever that you possibly can.

Think of the end result.

If you scrimp and save as much as humanly possible - you will finally end up a home *owner* with all the benefits that that entails.

Eventually, the mortgage *will* be paid off and you will enjoy a sense of financial freedom and self-confidence that is hard to describe.

And if you cream off 10-15% of your income before paying anything else and continue to invest as well as pay off your mortgage, you will without any doubt at all also be wealthy in time.

Don't forget, whatever the purchase price of your house originally, it's value will almost certainly have multiplied many times over by the time you pay off the mortgage. That's one bonus of the fixed rate mortgage.

By that time, you could very possibly be a millionaire!

Just One More Thing!

People often say that money doesn't bring happiness. Others say: "No, but it helps!" After all, creating wealth ultimately is about providing a life for yourself and your family that is devoid of financial worry.

Wealth usually means health, too. That's because when you are wealthy, your life is free of most of the negative stresses and strains that affect other people. It gives you a better chance of staying healthy.

Have you ever wondered what it *feels* like to be a millionaire? Maybe you should close your eyes for a few minutes each day and imagine how life would be for you.

Would it be that much different? You would still get up in the morning, go through each day attending to matters of the moment.

You would still have a bath or shower, get dressed and undressed, eat your meals, talk to friends and business associates, go to the movies, theatre, concerts and sports events.

So how would life be different? Other than the fact that you would be able to afford a bigger house, a better car, travel first class, eat and stay in five star establishments, easily be able to pay for your retirement and children's education and, if you or a member of your family fall ill, be able to afford the best medical care in a private hospital.

No matter how wealthy you become, you will almost certainly have as many happy days as disappointing, frustrating, worrying, plain awful days, all of which proves the fact that money isn't everything.

What money *does* give us is the sensation of well-being. And that perception is greatly enhanced by what is known as tithing.

The Joy of Tithing

Tithing goes back to biblical times and is one of the tenets of all the main religions. It is simply the act of *giving*.

The word tithe in Old English refers to one-tenth of something. In the 'olden days' that meant one-tenth of the land a farmer owned or of the produce he provided.

The idea of tithing is to give one-tenth of what you earn to others in need. In short, if you are blessed with riches, it was and still is perceived as your duty to help those less fortunate than yourself.

Today, we live in an era of shallowness and selfishness, and for all this self-centered approach to life, there is little to be gained from it.

You only have to look at the effects, now proven, of Facebook, Instagram and other social media. Young people who over-indulge in these practices all too often end up feeling depressed, even suicidal.

Tithing - giving voluntarily of your money, your time or your presence has precisely the opposite effect. Giving makes you feel fabulous! Because giving is a *joyful* process.

Of course, it is entirely up to you, but pretty much every wealthy person you will ever meet will tell you that by giving something back, life gives something indefinable back to you.

It's like the smile that you give out. It returns to you. Remember? When you give a portion of your wealth - or even before you have acquired wealth, in some strange way the Law of Attraction kicks in.

When you are generous with your wealth or give as much as you can, you will find that wealth in its various forms will come back to you.

You could say it makes you feel like a millionaire.

Why Not Start, Right Now?

So, do pledge right now to give to your favourite charities or good causes. Make it a Direct Debit. Even one pound a week is enough to start with. It can always be increased in time.

Most charities are online these days and you will find on their websites a very simple form to fill in for those who wish to set up an automatic and regular donation.

It is extremely easy to do this and, once the Direct debit is in place, you won't even miss the money.

But the knowledge that you are giving to those less fortunate than yourself or to people you meet and feel that you would like to help will truly make you feel great.

You will feel like a million bucks!

What Have You Learned in This Chapter?

1. That it is infinitely better to buy a house, however much it stretches your budget, than to rent.

2. To think of your monthly payments on a mortgage, not as a debt to be paid off, but as an investment in your future wealth.

3. The different types of mortgage.

4. Some ways of finding help with your initial deposit.

5. The costs associated with buying a house.

6. That you probably won't have to pay Stamp Duty.

7. That freehold is better than leasehold, but if you have to buy leasehold, make sure it is a *long* lease.

8. How much you *actually* pay the bank or mortgage lender when you buy a house.

9. Ways of paying off your mortgage early.

10. How to save money and cut the length of the length of a mortgage with bi-weekly payments.

11. To make absolutely sure that if you opt for bi-weekly payments, you must insist it goes to pay off your principal every two weeks and that the bank is not holding onto the money.

12. Not to become depressed by what may seem impossible. It's not! Think of No.2. on this list.

13. That giving to good causes makes you *feel* like a millionaire.

14. mortgage with bi-weekly payments.

15. To make absolutely sure that if you opt for bi-weekly payments, you must insist it goes to pay off your principal every two weeks and that the bank is not holding onto the money.

16. Not to become depressed by what may seem impossible. It's not! Think of No.2. on this list.

17. That giving to good causes makes you *feel* like a millionaire.

A Final Word

When I thought of the title for this little book, I was mindful of how easy it is to make money when you are young if you only know how.

It's sad, really, that I was never able to benefit from any financial advice myself - until my grandson, Peter, told me about Tony Robbins and his book, *Money - Master The Game.*

Peter turned my life around, although he doesn't really know it yet. So, I hope this little book will be a success because the contents are, as yet, still not taught in schools. They should be!

Everybody from the age of 15 up, should be aware of the power of compounding and the common sense of saving rather than spending.

I hope you persevere because it *is* worth it. It *is* possible. And if you have read this far, there is no doubt in my mind that you *can* do it! I wish you good fortune!

-£££-

... And a Few Word From The World's
Greatest Investors (and a couple of comics)

"School typically doesn't prepare young people for real life — unless their lives are spent following instructions and pleasing others. In my opinion, that's why so many students who succeed in school fail in life." - *Ray Dalio.*

"Opportunities come infrequently. When it rains gold, put out the bucket, not the thimble." - *Warren Buffett.*

"When you look at the results on an after-fee, after-tax basis, over reasonably long periods of time, there's almost no chance that you end up beating the index fund." - *David Swensen.*
"Money is better than poverty, if only for financial reasons" - *Woody Allen.*

"Diversify across securities, across asset classes, across markets and across time." - *Burton Malkiel.*

"Fund performance comes and goes. Costs go on forever." - *John C. Bogle.*

"Every professional in the City knows that index funds should be core building blocks in any long-term investor's portfolio." - *Jonathan Davis, The Spectator.*

"98% (of people) should really predominantly go into index funds, in my view. They have the most predictable outcomes." - *Charles Schwab.*

I practice Transcendental Meditation and believe that it has enhanced my open-mindedness, higher-level perspective, equanimity, and creativity. It helps slow things down so that I can act calmly even in the face of chaos, just like a ninja in a street fight." - *Ray Dalio.*

"The four most dangerous words in investing are: 'This time it's different'." - *Sir John Templeton*

"Be sure and diversify through low-cost index funds... And don't trade. Don't do something. Just stand there! No matter what! - *John C. Bogle*
"Sometimes life hits you in the head with a brick. Don't lose faith." - *Steve Jobs, late CEO, Apple.*

"Exposure from a young age to the realities of the world is a super-big thing." - *Bill Gates*

"The only limits to the possibilities in your life tomorrow are the 'buts' you use today." - *Les Brown.*

"A bank is a place that will lend you money if you can prove that you don't need it." - *Bob Hope.*

-£££-

BIBLIOGRAPHY

"Money - Master The Game' by Tony Robbins. Simon & Schuster UK Ltd.

"The Little Book of Common Sense Investing" by John C. Bogle - John Wiley & Sons, Inc, Hoboken, New Jersey.

"The Automatic Millionaire - A powerful one-step plan to live and finish rich" by David Bach

"The Intelligent Investor" by Benjamin Graham. Published by HarperBusiness 2003

"One Up on Wall Street" by Peter Lynch. Published by Simon & Schuster 2000

" How to Make Money in Stocks" by William J.Oneil. Published by McGraw-Hill, 2009.

Investor's Ultimate Guide from Novice to Expert: Invest Intelligently to Six Figures". By Jonathan S. Walker. Published by CreateSpace Independent Publishing Platform, 2017.

"Investing Demystified by Lars Kroijer. Published by FT Publishing International 2017.

"Money: Know More, Make More, Give More" by Rob Moore. Published by John Murray Learning 2017.

"Think and Grow Rich: The Original Classic" by Napoleon Hill/ Published by Capstone 2009.

"The Science of Getting Rich: The Original Classic" by Wallace Wattles. Published by Capstone 2010.

"Rich Dad , Poor Dad: What the Rich teach their kids about money that the poor and middle class do not" by Robert T. Kiyosaki. Published by Plata Publishing, 2017.

Morningstar
MoneySavingExpert.com (Martin Lewis)
Forbes Magazine
The Law of Attraction.com
The Telegraph Money Section
… and many more.